Fighting Squadron

Fighting Squadron

A SEQUEL TO DIVE BOMBER

Robert A. Winston

Naval Institute Press
Annapolis, Maryland

This is a facsimile edition of the book originally published in 1946 by Holiday House, Inc.

Library of Congress Cataloging-in-Publication Data

Winston, Robert A. (Robert Alexander), 1907–
    Fighting squadron : a sequel to Dive bomber / Robert A. Winston.
      p.   cm.
    Reprint. Originally published: New York : Holiday House, 1946.
    ISBN 1-55750-902-6
    1. Winston, Robert A. (Robert Alexander), 1907– . 2. World War,
1939–1945—Naval operations, American. 3. World War, 1939–1945—
Personal narratives, American. 4. World War, 1939–1945—Campaigns—
Pacific Area. 5. Fighter pilots—United States—Biography.
6. United States. Army Air Forces—Biography. I. Title.
D790.W5   1991
940.54′4973—dc20   90-23708

Printed in the United States of America on acid-free paper ∞

9 8 7 6 5 4 3 2

First printing

To My Wife

WHOSE COURAGE CARRIED ME THROUGH
AND WHOSE FAITH BROUGHT ME BACK

Foreword

THE OPINIONS AND ASSERTIONS contained herein are the private ones of the writer and are not to be construed as official or reflecting the views of the Navy Department or the Naval Service at large.

Some of the material in this book is reprinted through the courtesy of the *Saturday Evening Post,* whose kind permission is gratefully acknowledged.

ROBERT A. WINSTON
Guam, September 5, 1945

Contents

Fighting Squadron

Back in Harness

IN ALL MY LIFE I had never been so insulted as I was when it slowly dawned on me that Mr. Leroy Grumman was not going to let me fly his Hellcat fighter.

"Yes," he said, "it's a nice airplane, and we expect great things from it. Would you like to sit in the cockpit?"

That was the crowning blow. I had expected that he would ask me casually if I would like to *fly* the Hellcat. It wouldn't have been so bad if I hadn't flown all the way up from Washington on a cold February morning just to fly this particular airplane, at the express invitation of one of Mr. Grumman's assistants. Now it appeared that the assistant had been talking out of turn when he issued the invitation to me, for it was obvious that Mr. Grumman and his partner, Mr. Leon Swirbul, did not care to entrust their brand new "X" job to a part-time aviator who spent most of his days at a desk in the Navy Department.

To heap one insult on another, Messrs. Grumman and Swirbul assigned their chief test pilot, "Conny" Converse, to help me into the cockpit while the Hellcat sat in the hangar with the doors closed. Since Conny and I had been wing-mates in Fighting Squadron One on the old *Lexington* and had flown Navy fighters for years, this only rubbed salt in my wounded pride.

Conny sensed this as he stood on the wing while I sat in the cockpit.

"This cockpit's just right," he said. "Plenty of room, and no more hand cranks to raise the landing gear. Remember the old F3F, and what a strong right arm it developed? That's all gone—just move this lever, and the wheels retract hydraulically. She's got hydraulic gun chargers, too."

"Boy, what a gentleman's airplane!" I exclaimed. "How many guns?"

"Six fifties. Just touch those buttons with your toes, and your guns are all set. The bomb release is electric, too. Just press the button on the control stick."

"What size bomb?" I asked.

"Two thousand-pounders, or one and a belly tank," he replied.

"No! I don't believe it!"

"I'm not kidding," he said. "Remember, you've got two thousand horses pulling you now."

"That's right. I'd forgotten that big twin-row engine. Two thousand horsepower, and all for one man! It's hard to realize, after what we used to fly. Remember the old F4B-4?"

"Yes, and remember the first thousand-horsepower engines, and how we said they'd reached the all-time limit for single-seaters?"

"Golly," I said, looking at the wings. "This is a lot of airplane. What does she weigh?"

"Over six tons, gross load."

"No! Why, that's more than our twin-engined patrol planes weighed, only a few years back. Can it fly aboard with all that weight?"

"She makes the most beautiful carrier landings you ever saw."

"How about maneuverability? Remember, the Jap Zero only weighs about three tons."

"Yes, but the Zero has no self-sealing tanks or armor. Take a look at the armor plate behind you."

Behind the seat he showed me a broad plate of thick armor, and in front of me was a bullet-proof windshield. The Hellcat was literally a flying tank.

"She's pretty rugged," I admitted. "I'd give my eye-teeth to get into a squadron of these."

"So would I," said Conny with a sigh, "but I guess those days are gone forever."

"Oh, I don't know about that. I'm in just as good shape as I ever was."

He smiled indulgently. "I know. That's what I try to tell myself. But you notice that the young fellows like Bobby McReynolds get all the demonstration flight assignments. It's a young man's game. The British are taking their fighter pilots out of combat when they're past twenty-eight."

I took another long look at the Hellcat. "Well, just the same, I'm going to be flying one of these yet."

But it would take some doing.

ON THE FLIGHT back from Bethpage to Washington I flew over Floyd Bennett Field, where I had made my first solo flight as an aviation cadet eight years before. What had those eight years meant? A year of training in 1935, two years in fighter squadrons, 1936 on the west coast, and 1937 on the east coast with Fighting Squadron Six aboard the newly built aircraft carrier *Enterprise*. Then a year and a half as an instructor in fighters at Pensacola, to complete my four-year contract as an aviation cadet and get a commission as an ensign in the Naval Reserve in 1939. After that, a year of "inactive" duty as a test pilot in Finland, Belgium, and France during the German *Blitzkrieg* of 1940, then back to active duty at my own request in 1941, first as a flight instructor at Pensacola and then at Corpus Christi, still in fighters.*

Where had the war found me? On a desk job as aviation assistant to the director of naval public relations, because of newspaper experience prior to entering naval aviation. A fine job for a fighter pilot! Well, someone had to do the job, and I had the background. But why should I sit out the war, while all my friends in the Navy were out in the Pacific getting shot at? Only the week before, I had arranged a press conference for two Marine Corps pilots just back from Guadalcanal—Major John Smith, whom I had checked out in fighters at Pensacola in 1938, and Captain Marion Carl, who had served with me as an instructor at Pensacola a year ago.

* *Editor's Note:* The author's experiences during these years are described in DIVE BOMBER and ACES WILD.

These two men had really been fighting the war. Smith was the leading ace of the Marine Corps with twenty-six enemy planes to his credit, and Carl was not far behind him. Both had been shot down by Japanese Zeros and had gone up to fight again. Now they were home on leave, laden with combat decorations, while I sat safe and sound in an office chair in Washington. They had eyed me a bit curiously, as if wondering what was wrong with me, or what was keeping me out of the fight. Now I realized that in the eyes of the men who are doing the fighting, there will always be resentment of those who have not been assigned the unpleasant task of killing the enemy. No matter what any man contributes to a war effort, as long as he is physically fit and able to fight, returning veterans will always look at him with that curious expression which silently asks, *"How many of our enemies have you personally eliminated?"*

After all, this was a shooting war, and the only way to win it was to out shoot the Japs and the Germans. And those who were able to shoot, whether from a trench, a tank, a ship, or an airplane, would somehow get into action or would someday have to answer for themselves that silent question in the eyes of those who had shot and had been shot at.

With this realization the SNJ seemed to me to be creeping along through the air. My mind was made up. I was not too old for combat, no matter what anyone else might think. As soon as I could, I was going to get back into fighters—preferably Hellcats.

Back in the Navy Department, I marched straight up to the personnel office. At a desk marked "Naval Aviator Assignments" sat an old friend of mine, Lt. "Pete" Barrick. He and I had gone through flight training together at Pensacola at about the same time back in 1935, when the aviation cadet program was begun.

"Pete," I began, "could you use a pilot with nearly eight years of flying experience, most of it in fighters?"

"Sure we can," he answered. "Where is he now?"

"Right here. I want to get back into fighters."

"Wait a minute, Bob, aren't you getting a little old for fighters? How about a nice inshore patrol squadron?"

"Nothing doing. I'm ashore now. I want to go to sea. Besides, I instructed in fighters for nearly three years, and I could help someone form a squadron as the flight officer."

Pete eyed me skeptically for a moment, then glanced through his files. "Let's see," he mused. "You're a senior enough lieutenant to be executive officer of a squadron. Now, who needs an exec? Jim Sliney—no, he's got one. Here we are—Charlie Crommelin is forming a Hellcat squadron down at Norfolk. How would that suit you?"

"Fine! Perfect! Couldn't be better! I've known Charlie a long time. He was a gunnery instructor at Pensacola when we went through Squadron Five, remember?"

"That's right. Well, I'll put you down for that billet. How soon do you want to go?"

"Right away. As soon as you can write the orders."

"Got a relief?"

"Why, uh, no; but you can easily order someone else in my place."

"Not so fast. Secretary Gates set that job up. I can't write your orders until you get a release from him."

"Now, Pete, wait a minute. . . ."

"Nothing doing. Let me know when your relief is lined up, and then we can talk business."

That was that. After several days of frantic scouring around for a relief with a background in aviation public relations, we managed to steal Bob Neff from Pan American Airways and get him a commission as a lieutenant commander in the naval reserve. (He was stuck in Washington from then on, and still swears that he will never forgive me.)

Meanwhile I hightailed it down to Norfolk in an SNJ and sought out Lt. Comdr. Charlie Crommelin, who eyed me askance when I asked him if there was an opening in his Hellcat squadron.

"I don't think so, Bob," he said doubtfully. "I promised Eddie Owen I'd try to get him for my exec. You see, Eddie's been with me for the past year in the flight test section at Anacostia. Besides, you've been on duty in the Bureau for over a year, haven't you? How long have you been out of this dive and zoom business?"

"Over a year," I admitted, neglecting to add that I had not flown a fighter for over a year and a half.

"Why don't you take a refresher course?" he suggested. "My brother Dick is down at Jacksonville in the operational training center there. He's just back from combat and could give you a lot of good pointers."

Hiding my disappointment, I thanked him and flew back to Washington, where I again went to see Pete Barrick in the personnel office. Pete changed my orders, sending me to Jacksonville for the refresher course I requested. This was a lucky break for me. It nearly cost me my life a few weeks afterward, but it undoubtedly saved me from being shot down in my first combat later on.

First Crash

EARLY IN MARCH I reported to the Naval Air Station at Jacksonville, Florida, for a refresher course in fighters. Hunting up Lt. Dick Crommelin, I told him that his brother Charlie had sent me to him to get the latest word on fighter tactics.

Dick, who looked like all the rest of the five fighting Crommelin brothers, was the youngest of this family of naval officers. An older brother, Captain John Crommelin, was fitting out his own escort carrier, the newly built CVE *Liscome Bay*. "You've come just at the right time," Dick told me. "We're just starting this new refresher course—a school for prospective squadron commanders and executive officers. The idea is to give you all the latest dope we have, and to let you rub shoulders with some of the aces we've got here as instructors."

Among these instructors I soon found several old friends. Major Jack Dobbin, USMC, was just back from Guadalcanal. Lt. Comdr. Jimmy Thach was working on some training films of the fighter tactics he had developed as commanding officer of his own squadron, of which Lt. "Butch" O'Hare was a famous member. Lt.

"Doc" McCuskey, another old friend, was one of the gunnery instructors.

Other officers in this first group to take the new course were Lt. Comdr. Bill Collins and Lieutenants Charlie Ash, Marsh Beebe, and Ron Hoel. All of them were slated for fighter squadron billets. Bill Collins was getting his own squadron, with Charlie Ash as his executive officer. We were assigned to the auxiliary training station at Lee Field, which was the operational training center for fighter pilots, located just south of the main air station.

It was exhilarating to get back into single seaters after over a year of flying SNJ's on routine hops out of Washington. I was offered a choice of flying Corsairs or Wildcats.

"How about Hellcats?" I asked.

"Hellcats won't be available for several weeks," I was told. "If you start out in Corsairs, you'll be assigned to a Corsair squadron. If you train in Wildcats, you'll go to a Hellcat squadron."

"Then I'll take Wildcats," I answered, for I had my heart set on flying the Hellcat.

The little Wildcat was an easy plane to fly, with the usual roomy cockpit characteristic of all Grumman fighters, and excellent visibility. In a short time I felt thoroughly at home again in all the old maneuvers: slow rolls, Immelman turns, Cuban eights, and all of the aerobatics which helped me to smooth out my rusty airwork. After a few hours of this I started in on gunnery runs, firing at a towed sleeve target with wing guns instead of the synchronized fuselage guns I had used before.

There were many new wrinkles to fighter tactics, I soon discovered. Most unusual to me was the stepped-down formation, instead of the stepped-up formation which I had flown for years. This innovation was made necessary by the shift from airplanes of the earlier biplane type to the present low-wing and midwing designs. At first I found this a bit awkward, but soon got accustomed to the change in position and found that it had its advantages, including better visibility upward.

The old three-plane section had been supplanted by a four-plane division of two sections each. This was the most important single change in fighter tactics ever introduced, as it permitted the two sections to give each other mutual support when attacked, by means of the famous "Thach weave," a maneuver which had saved the lives of countless naval aviators in this war and which was later to save my own life. This protective maneuver, developed by Lt. Comdr. Jimmy Thach, was the essence of simplicity: pilots under attack merely turned toward their wingmen, so that the attacking plane would come under fire of at least one plane in the formation. If there were four planes in the formation, one section of two planes would act as a unit, turning toward the other section for protection. In enemy territory it was customary to weave in and out in a continuous series of turns, so that no opening would be given for enemy fighters to make an unopposed attack.

An electric reflector-type gunsight had replaced the

old telescope sight, with a new method for computing the target angle and the correct amount to "lead 'em like a duck." Synthetic training devices enabled us to practice gunnery on the ground, even to the extent of engaging in a very realistic mock dogfight in a fantastic contraption called a "Gunairstructor." A five-minute "flight" in this machine was a real workout which left us wringing wet, and which scored our percentage of hits on an electrical recorder. This was really training on a scientific basis. New safety devices included a shoulder harness which prevented the pilot's face from smashing into the plane's instrument panel in the event of a crash. This device undoubtedly saved my life one morning. I had taken off with a group of six other pilots to make dummy gunnery runs on a target plane flying at five thousand feet. We were making overhead runs on the target plane, starting from seven thousand feet, diving on the target and pulling back up into formation ahead of it. Being the senior pilot, I was leading the formation.

After the second run I glanced into my rear-view mirror to watch the plane behind me, and saw that the pilot was joining up with a great deal of excess speed which would make his plane go past mine. Banking quickly to one side, I watched him swish past me, much too close for comfort. Picking up my microphone, I cautioned him by radio: "Watch it, Number Two! You nearly hit me that time."

Since he did not answer, I resolved to watch out for myself, and after the next run I pulled out and glanced back over my shoulder to make sure I was out of his way. That backward glance was very nearly my last act in this life, for a second later the other plane hit mine with a tremendous, jolting crash that made me think the world itself had come to an end.

That one look behind me was all that saved my neck. The other plane, overtaking mine at terrific speed, would have smashed right through me if I had not been watching for it. As it was, I only saw it coming out of the corner of my eye, and realized instantly that it was going to hit me. Instinctively I had pushed over the stick, to nose down out of the way. Normally I would have pulled back on the stick and zoomed upward out of its way, or banked to one side as I had done to avoid it on the previous run. Either maneuver in this case would have been fatal, as I found later. The wing of the other plane had slashed through my plane's transparent cockpit canopy, smashing it so that it was jammed tightly closed, and breaking the goggles which I had pulled back over my forehead. The wing had then passed through my plane's propeller, jerking it loose and stopping the engine.

At the moment I did not know all this. All I knew was that the other plane had hit mine so hard that it momentarily jarred all the sense out of me. Fortunately the shoulder straps of my safety harness were in place and drawn tightly, otherwise I would have been knocked out by the force of the midair collision. (The other pilot was undoubtedly knocked unconscious, for he made no apparent effort to regain control of his plane. The other pilots watched it continue in a long, slanting glide that gradually steepened into a vertical dive from which it crashed and burned.)

I can still hear that rending crash, as his plane hit mine, and recall the frantic attempt I made to claw my way through the smashed canopy. The plexiglass canopy and windshield were starred so that I could not see out of the cockpit, which accentuated the feeling of being trapped. Releasing my safety belt, I shoved upward on the canopy until a section of it gave way, letting the blast of the slipstream in on my face. I pulled down my goggles, only to find that their lenses were broken.

Then I noticed for the first time that the plane was strangely silent except for the rush of air. Squinting through the hole in the canopy I saw that the horizon was in place and the plane in normal flying altitude. A quick glance at the instruments confirmed this: airspeed one hundred and eighty knots, turn-and-bank zero, altitude five thousand. I pushed the throttle. No response. Another squint outside and I saw the reason: the prop was frozen, with only part of one bent blade visible over the dented engine cowling. I moved the stick gently from side to side, and the Wildcat responded instantly. I eased it back and the airspeed slacked off normally. The rush of the wind died down and the blast in my face eased off as I pulled out of the glide to a level flight. Apparently the controls were undamaged. The Wildcat was cruising along at one hundred knots in a normal glide as if nothing were wrong with it at all.

I began to relax a bit from my panic. Plenty of altitude, several airfields around—maybe I could walk away from this yet. Setting the trim tabs so that I could use both hands, I tried to get back into my safety harness while I headed for the biggest open field I could see. The straps were too tight, but I managed to squirm back into the right shoulder strap and to lock the lap belt in place before I was down to two thousand feet, at which time I gave my full attention to the landing approach.

The field I had selected was an open pasture almost half a mile square, with plowed fields on three sides and pine woods at the north end. The wind was from the south. At eighteen hundred feet I started my turn into the wind. In keeping the nose well down, I picked up an extra twenty knots, and dropped my flaps to kill the excess speed. The field was directly in front of me, looking as smooth as a golf course. Before I realized it, I was lowering the landing gear. Then the bottom really dropped out of my glide. With a dead engine, the Wildcat settled like a stone toward the sixty-foot pine trees below me, and I saw I would never make the field.

Oh-Oh, I thought, *I should never have let those wheels down!*

There was a little clearing in the trees off to my left. I thought of trying for it, but years of flight training kept me from making the fatal mistake of attempting a sharp turn at low altitude. *Well, here we go!* I thought, and bracing my left hand against the instrument panel I eased back on the stick to kill as much speed as possible before I hit the trees. The Wildcat responded as if it were making a full-stall landing on a green carpet. There was a swish as it settled into the pine branches, then a progressive crashing which grew louder until it was a grinding, roaring, smashing, jolting sensation and sound combined, then dead silence and no more motion.

A hole had been torn in the canopy, just big enough for my head and shoulders. Tripping the catch on my safety belt, I plunged up through that hole, parachute and all. I heard the gasoline pouring from the smashed wing tanks, and smelled its odor strong in my nostrils. In a moment I was clear of the plane, which to my astonishment was crumpled up on one wing at the edge of the field I had never hoped to reach. Running as fast as I could go, I stopped only when I was well clear of the range of any gasoline explosion.

Nothing happened. There was no explosion, no fire. The wreckage of the plane just sat there, until I started to approach it cautiously. The propeller and nose section had been torn off and were sprawled out in front of the battered fuselage. Both wings were torn loose and bent back by the twelve-inch pine trunks they had slashed through. The plane had cut a swath through a dozen pine trees, and had uprooted and pushed over the last tree in its way, easing its fall to the ground. As I looked at the torn and twisted metal I wondered how anyone could have lived through such a crash. [See photograph.]

Only then did it occur to me that I was the one who had lived through that crash. I looked at my hands—only a few scratches. I felt my elbows, my shoulders, my knees—no broken bones, no apparent injuries. Suddenly I realized what I had escaped, and I heard myself shouting, "I'm alive! I'm *alive!*" until finally I had convinced myself that it was true.

Then I began to wonder why it was that I had been spared, and why I was not mangled up in that jumble of broken trees and torn metal. And suddenly the answer came to me like a great bright light, that it was not for myself that I had been spared, but for my wife and children, and I knelt down on my knees there in the grass and thanked God that He had spared me because of them.

My Own Squadron

AS I STOOD staring at the wreckage of the Wildcat a jeep bumped across the field and ground to a stop in front of me. In it were Lieutenant Commanders Eddie Konrad and Jack Lamade, who were also taking the refresher course at Lee Field.

"Are you hurt?" asked Eddie Konrad, as he jumped out of the jeep.

"Not a bit," I answered. "How about the plane that hit me?"

"It crashed and burned. The pilot didn't get out."

They drove me back to the air station dispensary where a doctor checked me over and painted a few scratches with iodine. "Come back in the morning," he told me, "and let me look you over again."

Marsh Beebe met me at the door. "Come along out to our hotel tonight," he invited me, "and we'll have a few beers and some stud poker."

I jumped at the suggestion, for I wanted to think about anything but that crash. Charlie Ash and his wife also joined us, and the evening passed before I realized it. Around midnight I went back to my room in B.O.Q.

completely relaxed, and slept soundly the rest of the night.

The next morning I awakened to find myself sore and stiff from a dozen bruised muscles I had not noticed the day before. After breakfast I limped over to the dispensary, feeling like the morning after the first day of football practice. The doctor was interested in only one thing.

"How did you sleep last night?" he asked.

"Like a log," I answered.

"Any dreams or nightmares?"

"Not a one."

"That's fine. Return to duty whenever you like."

That's all there was to it. No *Schneider* test, no psychological tests to worry about. I hurried on back to the hangar and asked the flight officer for a plane.

"Take it easy," he told me. "You can rest up a day or so and come back when you feel more like flying again."

This I did, but before the day was over I began to get restless and uneasy. The next morning I reported back to the flight officer and again asked for an airplane. This time I got it. The minute I was in the air all feelings of uneasiness and doubt left me. I put the Wildcat through every maneuver I could think of, and after an hour's workout I felt relaxed once more, feeling that the accident had not affected me.

The following day I was assigned to a new training squad, along with Bill Collins, Ron Hoel, Charlie Ash and Marsh Beebe. After a morning of gunnery practice we had lunch together and took off again in the afternoon for an hour of division tactics. Everything went smoothly, and we finished up the hour with a tail-chase and a simulated strafing attack on a nearby landing strip. Pushing over in a dive from ten thousand feet, we strung out in a loose column about fifty yards apart. I was next to last in the procession. We picked up a lot of speed in this dive, well over three hundred knots. The leader had already started his pull-out at about a thousand feet, when something went wrong. Suddenly I caught a glimpse of one of the planes ahead spinning like a top through half a dozen turns in a fraction of a second, then it simply disintegrated. It looked like another midair collision, but I could not tell how many planes were involved.

All of this happened so suddenly that I had no time to change course, and only by a narrow margin avoided flying through the wreckage. Easing out of the dive, I pulled off to one side, feeling weak and shaky. Below, on the airstrip at which we had been diving, was a flaming hulk, blazing away in a pool of oil. The rest of the wreckage was scattered all over the landscape. Over it buzzed the remaining planes of our group, futilely attempting to regain formation.

Wondering which of my friends it was whose lives had been snuffed out so suddenly, I stared resentfully at the oily black smoke which curled up from the blazing pyre below. Flying back alone, I landed and joined the group of pilots who waited with grim faces for each other's arrival. The only one missing was Charlie Ash.

There had been no collision; his plane had lost a wing in the pull-out and at that speed it had literally torn itself to bits. Bill Collins, who looked five years older than he had an hour before, broke the news to Charlie's wife. I could not keep the thought out of my mind that if there had been one more pine tree in my way only two days before, my own wife would now be a widow.

That night I found a message on my door to call the personnel office at the main station. Over the telephone I was informed that my orders had been modified: upon completion of my present duty I was to report to a newly commissioned fighting squadron as its commanding officer. My own squadron! I could not believe my ears, but when I drove down to get a copy of the orders I saw that it was true.

It is the goal of every pilot to have a command of his own, and to me the ultimate in desirability is command of a fighting squadron. But to get this as a lieutenant was almost unheard of. I mentioned this to a friend of mine who was on the training staff, another ex-cadet, Lt. Jim Patterson.

"Pat," I said, "there must be some mistake. They don't give squadrons to lieutenants, and as far as I know, no ex-cadet has command of a fighting squadron."

"You're right," he said, "but you won't take command as a lieutenant. You'll be a lieutenant commander!"

"No! You're kidding."

"I'm serious. There's an ALNAV coming out, and by the first of May you'll be trading those silver bars for a pair of gold oak leaves."

Pat was right. When I reported to my new station it was with another half stripe. My squadron was to be formed at the new Naval Air Station at Atlantic City, New Jersey. En route to report I stopped off at the Norfolk Naval Air Base for a refresher check-out in carrier landings aboard the U.S.S. *Charger*, an escort carrier used as a training ship in Chesapeake Bay. After flying aboard the big carriers, a landing on a CVE was a real sensation. I could hardly believe that airplanes could operate from a deck which looked from the air to be little longer than a shoebox. The arresting gear appeared to take up most of the flight deck, but after a few landings I decided that the deck was big enough at least for the Wildcat, and perhaps even for the SBD dive bombers. Then I saw a formation of Avengers circling overhead to enter the landing circle, and flew off shaking my head skeptically, thinking that the CVE designers had been much too optimistic.

A few days later I reported in at the Atlantic City Naval Air Station, passed an all-day flight physical examination for promotion, and assumed command of Fighting Squadron Thirty-One on May 1, 1943. There was not much to the squadron, but I was very proud of it. There were twelve officers on board, including the administrative officer, Lt. Joe Heffernan, who was an old friend from my home town of Washington, Indiana. We had not seen each other for over fifteen years.

The other eleven officers were naval aviators, all ensigns, all young, and fresh out of flight training. Their average age was about twenty-two. Most of them had completed two years of college before entering the Navy. Less than a third of them had received operational flight training. The youngest two of the group were married. Two others informed me that they were planning a double wedding the following weekend. A couple of others were toying with the idea of matrimony. After a few casual conversations with my pilots I felt a little behind the times. I also felt like a grandfather.

The squadron as yet had no airplanes. The hangars at the air station were barely completed and still full of loose lumber. Two of the airfield's main runways were still under construction. The unpaved roads of the air station were muddy ruts after even a light rain. Only one jeep was available for transportation, and that was assigned to the air group commander, Lt. Comdr. Joe Ruddy, USN.

Fortunately Joe Ruddy was no stranger to me. He had been stuck with me once before, when I was assigned to him as a student in Squadron Three at Pensacola in 1935. Now he again took me under his wing and got me off to a flying start. First he flew me down to Norfolk so that I could draw an airplane from the training pool. That gave me a choice of one airplane. I selected an SNJ, because I needed a two-seater. Flying it back to Atlantic City, I brought back one of my ensigns, checked out another SNJ, and together we flew the two airplanes back to our base. Then I flew back to Norfolk with another ensign who waited for me while I checked out in a Hellcat.

All this rigmarole may seem strange, to ferry training planes back and forth with qualified naval aviators as passengers, but the fact remains that I was afraid to trust these green kids to make this short flight unescorted, even with unlimited ceiling and perfect visibility. This reluctance on my part was not due to any doubts about the quality of their training, which I knew was the best in the world. All they lacked was good judgment, which would come only with experience. Discipline and example would help, but it is a peculiar quirk of human nature that most aviators learn their most important lessons only by somehow surviving mistakes which have been fatal to their less fortunate contemporaries.

My first flight in a Hellcat was an anticlimax and a disappointment. At Norfolk I had to take off from a small auxiliary field over a row of administration buildings under no-wind conditions. The plane was heavier than any fighter I had ever flown, and compared with the Wildcat it felt logy and sluggish on the take-off. The seat seemed too far back from the control stick, and the visibility was none too good even with the seat raised to its top limit. What I did not realize at this time was that the seat had been designed to hold a parachute with a pneumatic life raft and an emergency back pack which had not yet been issued, so that I was several inches too low in the seat and too far back from the controls.

The ensign who was to accompany me in the SNJ missed his assigned rendezvous point and altitude, but

I finally located him and led him back to the little municipal airport just outside of Atlantic City where we were parking our planes until our own runways were in commission. Here I formed my first good impression of the Hellcat, for it sat down easily on the small field with plenty of room to spare.

The next morning I called my eleven ensigns together for a heart-to-heart talk and laid all my cards on the table. I told them that we were going to have to train under conditions which were far from ideal, and asked their complete cooperation. I invited their comments, criticisms, and suggestions about every phase of our work together. I promised them all the wild flying they wanted, for our training syllabus would provide plenty of it, and begged them not to take any foolish chances on their own.

That afternoon two of them were killed doing the very things I had worried about and warned them against, just four days after the squadron had been commissioned.

I was certainly off to a fine start as a squadron commander.

Picking up the Pieces

OF COURSE the two ensigns who were killed on their
first flight in the squadron were the two who were planning the double wedding that weekend. And of course
each of them was the only child in the family. Their
sweethearts were already on the way to Atlantic City
for the double wedding, which made it even more difficult to break the news.

That one tragic accident, which meant heartbreak for
four families, was entirely unnecessary. That afternoon
we had all gone down together in a truck to the city
airport where our three airplanes were parked, kidding the two who were to be married about their forthcoming honeymoons. By mutual consent of the others,
they were voted the honor of making the squadron's
first flight. This was to be an hour of instrument practice
in one of the SNJ's, with explicit instructions to stay
close to the field and to avoid stalls, wingovers and other
instrument training maneuvers under five thousand
feet. Two other ensigns were assigned to the remaining
SNJ for a similar flight in a different area.

After the instrument flights took off I gathered the re-

maining pilots around the Hellcat for a cockpit check-
out. Half an hour later Joe Ruddy flew in from Norfolk
with a Grumman Avenger, the first of his TBF's. Everyone paused to watch it come in, then we went back to
our Hellcat. Ruddy parked his TBF, checked in at the
airport operations office, and strolled over to see how
we were making out.

"By the way," he said, "the airport manager just had
a phone call about a plane down about ten miles west of
the air station. You haven't got any planes out that way,
have you?"

"I've got two instrument flights out," I replied, "but
they're not in that area."

"Maybe it's an Army plane from Millville."

Just then one of the SNJ's approached for a landing.
When the pilot arrived I asked him if he had seen our
other SNJ during his flight.

"Yes, sir, I saw him about half an hour ago over the
air station," he answered.

"How high was he and which way was he going?" I
asked.

"About a thousand feet, I believe. As I recall, he was
heading west."

Joe Ruddy glanced at his watch. We eyed each other
silently. I felt a sinking feeling in my stomach. Jumping
into the SNJ, I took off and headed west, hoping that
I would not find what I knew I was going to find. When
I found the scene of the crash, one look was enough to
know that there was no longer any need to hurry. The
wreckage was scattered for a hundred yards, with noth-

ing left but bright bits of twisted dural. There had been no fire, but the airplane had obviously struck the ground at terrific speed, barely missing a farm house.

The details of the accident were as discouraging and disappointing as they were depressing. The pilots of both SNJ's had disobeyed all their instructions. Instead of practicing instrument work they had engaged in a wild dogfight over the air station and had then buzzed the field at low altitude. The plane which crashed was observed by witnesses on a golf course to be flying upside down at about five hundred feet, from which altitude it lost a wing and crashed. A close inspection of the remaining SNJ showed that it also had been overstressed almost to the point of structural failure. Its main spar was bent so badly that the plane was no longer safe even for normal flight, and had to be turned in for a major overhaul. We had very nearly lost four pilots instead of two.

When I pointed this out to the two survivors they looked sick and frightened, and as an additional object lesson I assigned them the duty of preparing the official inventory of the deceased pilots' personal effects for shipment to their bereaved families.

That left the squadron with nine ensigns and one airplane. Four new ensigns reported aboard later that week, and ferry pilots began bringing in more Hellcats until we had our full complement of twelve fighters. The rest of the air group was a composite squadron of nine SBD Douglas Dauntless dive bombers and nine TBF Grumman Avenger torpedo planes.

With thirteen ensigns I was rapidly approaching the squadron's complement of sixteen pilots without the experienced officers so essential to any well-balanced squadron. One of the newly reported ensigns took off in an SNJ in a 20-knot breeze down-wind, caromed off a concrete mixer, and crashed into an automobile full of workmen, who saw him coming and bailed out just in time to save their necks. Luckily no one was injured, but the plane and car were demolished. I transferred the pilot to an inshore patrol squadron where he would have wind-streaks on the water to show him which way the wind blew. Another ensign joined him after nosing up two Hellcats in rapid succession by careless taxiing.

Shortly after these incidents an enlisted aircrewman ran out from behind a row of airplanes in front of one of my ensigns who was taxiing a Hellcat and was struck by its propeller, which killed him instantly. My pilot was absolved of any responsibility, but I began to feel like a mother duck with a brood of chicks.

Appealing to COMAIRLANT's personnel officer, I requested half a dozen more experienced pilots. This was granted. Among others I obtained Lt. "Pat" Patterson from the Jacksonville training base for an executive officer, and recruited two experienced former enlisted pilots, Lieutenants (jg) Jack Wirth and "Push" Scales, as division leaders. With these older men to help train the young ensigns, the squadron rapidly began to round into good shape.

One advantage of a small squadron was that I was able to fly with each pilot until I knew his individual flying habits. I not only tried out each pilot as wingman, but I also flew wing on each man in the squadron. Our succession of unnecessary accidents had taught me that these wild young ensigns could be kept in line only by means of some incentive which appealed to them. Mine was a "mustang" squadron, with not one Naval Academy graduate in the whole outfit. Since they did not plan to remain in the Navy as a career, the threat of disciplinary action was no more of a deterrent to their reckless impulses than the obvious dangers of stunting at low altitude had been.

The one way I could keep them in line was by competition. They all loved to fly more than anything else in the world, and they all wanted to fly fighters—preferably Hellcats. The only threat that meant anything to them was that of being transferred to some other branch of flying. Our training command, well aware of this situation, assigned three or four additional pilots to each carrier squadron, so that no individual pilot could be sure he had made the grade until the extra pilots had been turned in at the end of the training period. This competition kept the boys on their toes, and made for better gunnery and bombing scores.

Gradually the individual personalities began to assert themselves. Volumes could be written about each man, but for the purposes of this account I will list only a few individuals whose exploits are noted in later chapters: Ensigns Nooy and Bowie, whose names are pronounced alike, flew with me in the first division, along with Bob Wilson, who was the leader of the second section. (Four planes of two sections each made up a division; three such divisions made a twelve-plane squadron.) Pat Patterson's wingman was a lanky Texan named A. R. Hawkins, "Hawkeye" for short. Jack Wirth led Pat's second section, with a skinny youngster named Frank Hayde for his fourth man.

Only a few weeks after my arrival Joe Ruddy was transferred to the U.S.S. *Ranger* as the carrier's air officer. His relief was Lt. Comdr. Jim Vredenburgh, a Naval Academy graduate who had just come from command of an inshore patrol squadron. His executive officer was Lt. E. E. Wood, and his biggest torpedo-plane pilot was Lt. (jg) J. B. Russell, a two-hundred-and-twenty-pound extrovert known as "The Beast," who enthusiastically took over his self-assigned duties as the air group's permanent master of ceremonies.

The commanding officer of our ship was a red-headed naval aviator who loved to fly, Captain Malcolm F. Schoeffel, USN, who flew down regularly from Philadelphia to advise and assist us. Our ship, a light carrier of the *Independence* class, was the U.S.S. *Cabot,** one of the nine such carriers converted from *Cleveland*-class cruisers to meet the urgent need for aircraft carriers after the Battle of Midway had shown that from now on we could expect carrier warfare instead of sur-

* *Editor's Note:* The *Cabot* was the ship on which the late Ernie Pyle wrote his famous series of columns about aircraft carriers en route to the invasion of Okinawa, during which he met his death on Ie Shima. The *Cabot,* which was named after a famous commerce raider of the Revolutionary War, was later nicknamed "The Iron Woman of the Fleet" in honor of her combat record.

face naval engagements. The *Cabot* was commissioned
at the Philadelphia Navy Yard, and while her trial runs
were being held the air group flew up to the Naval Air
Station at Quonset Point, Rhode Island, for joint Army-
Navy maneuvers. Here we lost another pilot, who spun
in from three thousand feet when he tried to follow an
Army fighter which had made a practice run on him.

At Quonset we also met Rear Admiral Calvin T.
Durgin, a naval aviator in charge of carrier training,
who helped us through our growing pains and was like
a father to the squadron. He helped us select a squadron
insignia, which at first we cluttered up with a lot of
heraldic motifs, but finally trimmed down to a winged
meataxe, symbolic of the Hellcat with all its fire-power,
and the motto: "cut 'em down!"

Shakedown Cruise

THERE WAS ONE FLIGHT which I had to get out of my system before leaving the country, and that was a return visit to the Grumman plant in a Hellcat. A good excuse for such a trip came up when we needed some engineering data on fuselage modifications. Flying to Long Island, I circled the Grumman plant at Bethpage, waiting for a landing clearance. As I looked down on the little group of buildings in the middle of Long Island's fertile farms I reflected that not so long ago a few Grumman Wildcats on Guadalcanal had prevented the Japanese conquest of that island and the otherwise inevitable invasion of Australia. Other Grumman planes had helped turn the tide at the Battle of Midway, on which the fate of Western civilization probably hinged.

Now we had a new Grumman fighter, thanks to the enterprise and hard work of the men in the factory below me, backed by the foresight and faith of the Navy's airplane designers. Here I was, sitting safely and comfortably in an airplane worth almost a hundred thousand dollars. The engine ticking over in front of me bore a Pratt & Whitney trademark, with the slogan "Dependable Engines." What an understatement! In nine years of flying for the Navy, I had never had an engine failure.

A call from the airfield control tower interrupted my reflections: "Hello, Navy zero four nine four three from Grumman Tower, you are clear to land."

As I taxied up to the line Conny Converse walked out to meet me. "I saw your name on the departure report," he said, grinning. "I see they couldn't keep you out of the Hellcat!"

Conny gave me all the latest dope I needed, took me out to lunch, and sent me on my way satisfied. Mr. Grumman was much too busy building airplanes to worry about who flew them, but my triumph was no less complete, for I had proved to my own satisfaction that I was not too old for fighters, and now had my own Hellcat squadron.

A few days later we made our carrier qualification landings aboard the *Cabot* in Chesapeake Bay. Those first few landings were a bit ragged, for we all felt jittery about landing aboard a CVL, which has a narrower flight deck than even the CVE class of carriers.* However, all went well except for a few blown-out tires, and after the last airplane was aboard the *Cabot* she nosed out through the submarine nets to start her shakedown cruise. At first we headed east for several hours, and

---

* *Editor's Note:* There were three sizes of carriers in action at this time: the big *Essex*-class carriers, known as CV's; the light carriers, or CVL's, converted from *Cleveland*-class cruisers; and the CVE's, or escort carriers, which were not used in the fast carrier task forces because of their limited cruising speeds.

everyone commented on the smoothness with which the ship rode the big groundswells. Everything aboard was as neat and clean as only a new ship can be. "What a dream ship!" was the general comment.

After dinner in the airy wardroom several of us went up to the air-conditioned ready room for a few hands of stud poker. We were still heading east, and could feel the gentle rise and fall of the ship as it headed into the swells. A bit later we could feel that we were turning to starboard.

"Well, we're heading south toward Cape Hatteras," observed Jack Wirth.

The ship gave a few gentle preliminary rolls as she turned broadside to the wind, then we felt her rise on a larger wave. First she rolled heavily to port, then violently to starboard. Card table, chairs, players, and poker chips slid across the room and rolled together in a confused pile.

"Whoopee!" yelled Push Scales. "There goes your dream ship out the porthole!"

From that time forward, we learned that if the wind blew, the *Cabot* would roll. The next morning we reached smoother water. Our destination was Trinidad, where the land-locked Gulf of Paria would give us a maneuvering area safe from the German submarines which were operating along the Atlantic trade routes. Escorting us were two destroyers, their depth-charges ready and their underwater listening gear continuously alert for any U-boats which might be lurking along our route. By day our own air group flew a constant anti-submarine patrol, and at night all port covers were dogged down to prevent even the slightest glimmer of light from showing.

The ship's executive officer was Commander "Gat" Washburn, USN, also a naval aviator. Two ex-cadets who had been through Pensacola with me were in the Air Department, Lieutenant Commanders Al Gurney and Al Masters. We had two crackerjack landing signal officers, Lt. Bill Hall and Ensign Bill Green. To watch them bring our pilots aboard was a real treat, for they were just about the best L.S.O.'s in the business.

To watch the airplanes come aboard, however, was an ordeal which I dreaded. I would rather make fifty carrier landings myself than watch five new pilots fly aboard. Our fighters usually landed first after our air group maneuvers, which meant that I was usually first aboard. After landing I would go up to the rear of the open bridge to watch the rest of the planes land. From this point I could watch every phase of a bad approach and could see what mistakes were being made from the time a pilot made his first error until his plane either rolled off the deck into the gun galleries, smashed into the steel barrier cables directly beneath me, or spun in astern of the ramp. On our shakedown cruise I saw such accidents happen several times.

The accidents were actually more of a relief than the narrow escapes, for in most cases we could look right down into the cockpit and see that no one was injured. But sometimes a Hellcat or an Avenger would get a waveoff after a bad approach and would pull up at a steep angle, barely missing the ramp and forcing the L.S.O. to dive for his safety net or run for dear life across the flight deck, while the plane would stagger along ready to stall in at any moment, bouncing its landing hook across the arresting gear or through the gun mounts, barely missing the barriers or the parked planes beyond, until every man on the flight deck gasped with relief to see it finally clear the last obstruction by a matter of inches. Once while I was standing beside Captain Schoeffel on the open bridge an Avenger came so close to knocking a parked Hellcat down into an open elevator shaft upon a group of plane handlers that we turned to each other tense and speechless, each with a hand over his palpitating stomach.

Another time we both ducked as the wing of an Avenger splintered against the bridge railing beside us, fifteen feet above the flight deck, while the big plane sailed on to crash down upon the forward twin 40-mm. gun mount on the starboard side, where it toppled off upside down into the sea. We rushed across the bridge to see the pilot and crew climb out spitting salt water while our plane-guard destroyer hove to and hauled them aboard. Again no one was hurt, unbelievably.

En route to Trinidad we practiced coordinated attacks, using a spar towed behind the ship as a target. The SBD's dropped practice bombs, the fighters strafed with their fixed guns, and the Avengers dropped water-filled bombs in lieu of torpedoes. Part of the time we flew our planes off the flight deck, and on other occasions we were catapulted from the deck. The catapult

was a thrill at first, but we soon came to prefer it as an
easier and safer method of take-off, especially at night.
One advantage of a catapult take-off is that we were
always sure of clearing the deck, for even with a dead
engine the catapult had enough power to throw the
plane clear. One of our Avenger pilots was the unwilling
guinea pig for an unscheduled test which resulted in this
discovery, when through a mixup of signals the catapult
was fired before he could open his throttle. The Avenger
trickled off the flight deck with enough speed to miss
the ship's forecastle below, and while we saved the
plane crew we lost the airplane.

One day I had an exceptionally close call while landing aboard. Using too long an approach, I over-shot my
turn and Bill Hall gave me a waveoff. As I opened the
throttle to pull clear I saw the ramp rising beneath me
when the ship nosed down between swells, and felt my
body surge forward against the shoulder straps of my
safety harness. There is the same feeling when the arresting gear begins to take hold during a normal carrier
landing. At once I knew that my tail hook had engaged
one of the arresting cables. I had "caught a wire on a
waveoff"—a predicament which has resulted in a large
number of fatal carrier landing accidents.

The usual sequence of such an accident is that the
pilot jams on full throttle until the arresting cable pays
out to full length and drags the plane down, either pulling the fuselage apart or throwing the airplane over the
side of the ship. Having seen several accidents of this
nature, I had observed that the more power the pilot

put on, the harder the arresting cable yanked the plane down. Full power only made the resulting crash more violent.

As soon as I felt the gear grab my tail hook, I instinctively chopped my throttle back and attempted to make a normal landing. To my amazement and intense relief, the Hellcat did just that. I looked back to find that I had caught the first wire, which had paid out to its full length without breaking and was now stretched out so tightly behind me that when I released my brakes it began to haul my plane backward.

This experience worried me. At first I began to fear that I was losing my touch, that perhaps I really had been out of fighters too long. This feeling of doubt grew on me until I felt certain that I would soon be killed in a carrier landing accident. I wrote a final letter of instructions addressed to my roommate regarding the disposition of my personal effects and left it with all my ready cash in the ship's safe. For several days after this experience, each carrier landing that I made was a mental ordeal for me. Every time the L.S.O. gave me the signal to cut my throttle I would head for the center of the barriers and hope for the best; if my hook missed a wire, the barriers would stop me. This proved to be such a good system that I had the rest of the squadron adopt it, with a resultant decrease in bent propellers and blown-out tires. My confidence returned with the completion of each successful flight until I again enjoyed making carrier landings. To this day, however, I still experience a feeling of mild surprise to find myself

safely aboard after a carrier landing, and I always concentrate on each approach as if it were my last chance.

ONE MORNING we went up on the flight deck to see
towering mountain peaks rising above the southern horizon—our first glimpse of South America. That morning, with a safe harbor in sight, we lost another pilot
through an accident which should never have happened. One of my ensigns loved to bet on anything—
five dollars on the turn of a card, how soon it would rain,
which one of two flies on a table would take off first—
anything with an element of doubt. He always had a
pocket full of loose five-dollar bills. This morning he was
accompanying one of our Avengers on anti-submarine
patrol. He spotted something—a whitecapped wave, a
school of fish or a clump of seaweed—and swerved im-
petuously to investigate it without first indicating his
intentions to the Avenger's pilot. At that moment the
Avenger was starting a turn at the completion of one leg
of its search. The two planes collided, and the Avenger's
propeller cut off the Hellcat's tail.

The ensign in the Hellcat had plenty of altitude to
bail out, but crashed with the airplane into the sea near
the entrance to the Gulf of Paria known as the Dragon's
Mouth. The Avenger staggered back aboard with a bent
propeller. I was later informed that my ensign had been
in the habit of flying with his parachute harness unfas-
tened, because it was too hot and uncomfortable in the

tropical sunlight. Whether or not he had gambled his life away we will never know, but later on in Trinidad I heard a peculiar sequel to this tragedy, when I happened to run into the officer who had been in charge of the crash boat which had sped out to the accident.

"You won't believe this," he warned me, "but when we arrived on the spot the water was clear and glassy smooth, so that we were able to pick up everything which remained after the crash. We found the usual junk—a seat cushion, an oxygen bottle, various bits of cork and such, and right in the middle of the oil slick, floating on top of the water, we picked up two crumpled five-dollar bills!"

The rest of our shakedown cruise was uneventful, except for a few routine alerts on the return trip whenever our escorting destroyers reported a possible under- water submarine contact. Upon our return we were informed that a drastic change was being made in the composition of CVL air groups. The SBD, long the dependable workhorse dive bomber of the earlier carrier battles, was being replaced by the SB2C Curtiss Helldiver, a larger airplane too big for the narrow flight decks of CVL's like the *Cabot*. The Helldivers were being assigned to the big *Essex*-class carriers, and the CVL air group complements were being changed. That meant goodbye to our nine SBD's, and doubling our fighter squadron. The big question was, with only a few weeks to go before we were scheduled to leave for the Pacific, where were we going to find sixteen more Hellcat pilots who were ready for combat?

Again it was Admiral Durgin who came to our assistance. Fighting Squadron Forty-Three, training near Quonset, was almost ready for its shakedown cruise. Lt. Comdr. Bill Coleman, who had formed and trained the squadron, was senior enough for a larger command. His pilots were transferred to my squadron, and we were assigned twelve new Hellcats. We spent our last few days ashore getting the new pilots checked out in carrier landings aboard the U.S.S. *Charger* at Norfolk. During their qualification landings two of the new pilots caught a wire after a waveoff. One, a newly married ensign, poured on the coal, pulled his Hellcat in two, and went over the side strapped in the cockpit. He never had a chance to get out. The other, a senior lieutenant and experienced pilot named Doug Mulcahy, realized that he had hooked a wire, chopped his throttle and ended up in the catwalk. Again experience meant the difference between life and death.

One other pilot who qualified aboard the *Charger* was so tense that when I watched him as he landed aboard the *Cabot* I recommended that he be held over for further training. He was bitterly disappointed at being left behind while his friends went off to fight, and I suppose he hated me for trying to save his neck, just as every pilot whom I had transferred took it as a personal insult regardless of the circumstances. He crashed fatally not long afterward, but not on our ship.

About the middle of November we flew aboard the *Cabot* off Nantucket and headed south again, this time for the Panama Canal. En route we trained intensively, modifying our tactics to meet the changes in our air group organization. The first thing I did was to reorganize each four-man team in the fighter squadron to include both old and new pilots, so that no cliques could get started. This gave me a balanced organization.

"We're not going to have any first team," I told them. "Each division should be as good as any of the others. Each pilot must be as good as any other in the division, so that he can take over the lead of his section, division, or squadron, or the whole air group at any time. Each wingman will take his turn at leading, so that if the senior pilot can't start his engine or has a radio failure any man in the squadron can take his place."

The ensigns quickly responded to this added responsibility, which also kept the older pilots on their toes. By the time we had passed through the Canal into the Pacific, my boys were beginning to look like fighter pilots. One morning I was very much pleased to be able to post a note from Captain Schoeffel on the ready room bulletin board which read as follows:

THE WAY IN WHICH THE PILOTS ARE CUTTING CORNERS AND CLOSING UP THE INTERVALS IN LANDING OPERATIONS IS VERY GRATIFYING. FURTHER IMPROVEMENT IS OF COURSE POSSIBLE, BUT I AM WELL PLEASED WITH THE RESULTS YOU HAVE OBTAINED SO FAR. PLEASE REALIZE, HOWEVER, I SHOULD NEVER BE "SATISFIED" UNLESS THE GROUP COULD LAND IN FORMATION.   —M.F.S.

Pearl Harbor

AS THE *Cabot* threaded her way carefully through the dredged channel into Pearl Harbor we all lined the flight deck watching for marks of the infamous Japanese sneak attack which had plunged the United States into the Second World War. By this time most of the wreckage had been cleared up, except for the salvaging operations which were still progressing on the old target battleship *Utah* and the battered hulk of the *Oklahoma*. However, there still was a gummy black stripe at the high tide mark around all the piers and pilings where fuel oil from our battered ships had left an indelible mourning band on Pearl Harbor's waterfront.

Most significant of anything we saw as the *Cabot's* big anchor chain rattled down was that Pearl Harbor was almost empty of warships. Except for our own ship and one CVE, not another carrier was to be seen. The usual tugs and freighters were present, but the big piers where the giant carriers and battlewagons were usually berthed were now deserted. The Fleet was out.

As soon as the realization dawned on us a wave of disappointment swept the ship, for we soon found what this meant: the long-expected invasion of the Gilbert Islands was under way, and we had just missed getting in on it. This situation had its advantages, for we had our pick of all the training bases and facilities in the Hawaiian area to polish up our combat tactics before going into action. In addition, it was heartening to know that our Navy was at last on the offensive after two years of desperate last-ditch defensive holding operations which at one time whittled our aircraft carrier strength down until we had only one operational carrier left in the Pacific—the bombed and battered *Enterprise*.

Now our Navy had enough carrier strength to cover offensive operations of its own, thanks to the big new *Essex*-class giants and the swift, maneuverable converted cruisers like the *Cabot*. It was comforting to know that we were no longer outnumbered three or four ships to one, as the Japs had outweighed us during the battle off the Santa Cruz Islands only a year before. In looking back on it now, it is hard to realize how narrowly we escaped losing Australia, the Hawaiian Islands and Alaska to the Japanese, or how much we owe to our aircraft carriers in preventing these invasions.

At that time my own reactions and those of the rest of our pilots were typical. Each of us was trying to guess where the Navy would strike next. Poring over a big chart of the Central Pacific which showed airline distances between various Jap-held bases, we argued the possibilities.

"I'll bet we take Wake Island back next," observed one pilot.

"No, it's too far north," answered another. "We'll probably go on down and help MacArthur out around Rabaul."

This idea was hooted as too fantastic: "Near all those big land bases? Why, they'd blow us out of the water!"

"How about the Marshalls? They'll be just as tough as the Gilberts. Did you hear how they butchered our Marines at Tarawa?"

"Brother, it's *all* gonna be tough!"

"I hope we can by-pass some of those islands like Kwajalein, they say it's really loaded for bear."

"Oh, they'd never go there; Kwajalein's the biggest atoll in the world."

Lt. Push Scales took a long hard look at the map. "I don't care where they take us," he said slowly, "as long as we keep away from *Truk*. I'd rather see us sail right up Tokyo Bay than go anywhere near Truk!

That was one point on which our agreement was unanimous. Truk would have to be by-passed; no carrier task force could ever risk itself near this Japanese equivalent of Pearl Harbor.

This was a logical conclusion, for after we had flown from Ford Island to one after another of the big Hawaiian airfields and had seen the area's tremendous air strength and intricate warning system, anything even remotely comparable to it was impregnable as far as we were concerned, and we wanted no part of it. Thus we dismissed the possibility of a carrier strike on Truk.

At ComAirPac staff headquarters I went to see an old acquaintance who had always been a fatherly adviser,

Commander "Spig" Wead, who later received the Legion of Merit for his outstanding work in a position of great responsibility. He had previously been on the retired list for nearly a dozen years, after an accident left him with injuries which would have made any other man give up in despair, but which in his case only seemed to double his zest for hard work. Commander Wead answered my request for advice with an invaluable tip: "Get all the night work your pilots can stand, especially night take-offs and joinups. The longer this war lasts, the more night flying you'll see."

Following this sound advice, I arranged for the air group to be transferred to a large outlying base where the runways were down close to the water, and sent in a flight schedule which made the air station operations officer groan when he saw it.

"What's the matter, does the light hurt your eyes?" he asked testily. "You'll keep everybody on the station awake with this night-owl schedule."

This proved to be only good-natured grousing, for we got the best of service from the local CASU, which kept our planes in commission, our guns in good shape, and provided us with all the towed targets we could shoot at. Pat Patterson and I then put our heads together and worked out a flight schedule which gave us plenty of night work in addition to an intensive refresher course in gunnery and bombing, working in shifts so that each pilot had plenty of time for rest and recreation even though the squadron flew seven days a week. During this period we flew back aboard the carrier for several short refresher cruises, passing our qualification inspections with flying colors.

Training at the same base with us was Commander N. M. ("Bus") Miller, who had a squadron of four-engined Liberators. We cooked up a deal whereby our fighters could make runs on his planes if we would tow targets for his gunners to shoot at. This was invaluable experience which later paid off for both squadrons.

In January the carriers began to straggle in from the invasion of the Gilberts, and we eagerly sought out the various pilots we knew to inquire about the latest Japanese tactics and the best means of countering their offensive or defensive maneuvers. I ran into Harry Harrison, now a lieutenant commander with a squadron of his own, in the officers' club at Kaneohe. He informed me that Commander Charlie Crommelin had been wounded by Japanese anti-aircraft fire during a low altitude photographic flight. Charlie's plane had been hit in the windshield by an explosive projectile which shattered the canopy and filled his face with hundreds of fragments, temporarily blinding him in one eye. In spite of this he succeeded in flying his Hellcat back aboard for a perfect landing, and was now recuperating in a hospital. His older brother, Captain John Crommelin, had suffered severe burns when his carrier, the *Liscome Bay*, had exploded and sunk after being torpedoed by a Jap submarine, but he was already up and around. Also on the *Liscome Bay* was my old friend Marsh Beebe, who had been trapped below when the blast came, but who also lived to fight again.

Harry Harrison gave me plenty of tips from his own experiences in the Gilberts and from previous strikes in the Marshall Islands.

"Mili is a hot spot," he said, "and so is Wotje, but the worst hornets' nest I've seen is Kwajalein. Stay clear of there, or they'll shoot your pants off."

Other good advice came from Lt. "Boogie" Hoffman, an experienced old-timer who had done most of the comparative test flights in the first captured Jap Zero which was salvaged intact. He also warned us about the Jap fighters at Kwajalein, in a play-by-play description which held the assembled squadron spellbound.

"You've got to stick together at all times," he told us, "or they'll gang up on you and chop you down one at a time. You all know Eddie Owen, who was in the Navy's fighter test section at Anacostia and one of the best fighter pilots in the Fleet. Well, here's what happened to Ed when his wingman got lost: we were strafing planes on the ground at Roi airfield, starting our dives from about ten or twelve thousand feet. The field was covered with Bettys and Zeros, nearly a hundred planes, with their engines turning over. Ed had started down to strafe when he saw a Hellcat with two Zeros on its tail. He cut in behind the procession and shot down one of the Zeros. This happened at the edge of a cloud layer which was full of Zeros, and they were definitely first-string pilots. Going through the edge of this cloud layer, Ed's wingman was straggling behind too far and lost contact. Ed went on down and knocked off another Jap, and then zoomed back up to look for his wingman.

"On the way back he was jumped by four or five Zeros who really worked him over until his plane was riddled. He finally managed to dive away from them and limped back with one aileron shot away, his rudder controls almost gone, his engine smoking and vibrating, and his radio and instruments shot out. His engine quit just as he got over the carrier, and with no controls he had to bail out. He was picked up by a destroyer, and considers himself lucky to be alive.

"My own division was cruising along southeast of Roi at about four thousand feet when we saw a big bunch of Zeros, fifteen to twenty planes, diving on us from astern, dropping their belly tanks on the way down. We immediately went into a defensive weave, but there were too many of them and they knew their business too well. Each time we swung to the outside of a turn they would hit us. Each time we would weave we would get in short snap shots at them, but we were pulling so many G's in such tight turns at high speed that my guns jammed, one after another, until I had only one gun firing. The action was so violent that I couldn't relax for an instant, not even long enough to touch my hydraulic gun chargers, even with one foot.

"We knew we were hitting them, but we couldn't take time out even to see if they flamed or splashed, for they were all over us. Then my wingman got hit. First they set one of his wing tanks afire, and then the other. Then he dropped down out of control with both wing tanks burning. He didn't get out." He paused here, his eyes glistening at the recollection, then went on. "You feel pretty bad when you lose your wingman, and he was the best wingman I ever saw. Well, we finally worked our way back toward the ship and gradually pulled away from the yellow devils. That old "Thach weave" saved our necks, beyond any doubt. If we had ever separated with that mob on our tails, not one of us would ever have gotten back.

"Now you can see our mistakes. First, Ed and I should have kept our two divisions together, in which case the Zeros would probably never have attacked us. At least we could have defended ourselves. Also, if we had stuck together we could have worked over all those Bettys on the airfield and saved ourselves a lot of grief later, for that night *they* worked *us* over, in a torpedo attack that lasted nearly eight hours. Butch O'Hare and Johnny Phillips took off in the dark and shot some of them down, but Butch is missing and presumed lost. So, take it from one who learned from sad experience: *stick together,* and never break up your division under any circumstances."

This sound advice made a big impression on all of us, and together with other tactical tips which Hoffman gave us, particularly on strafing technique, it was incorporated into the squadron's combat doctrine.

In rounding out our Hawaiian training we made several trips to the island of Maui and Hawaii, flying along between the snow-capped peaks of Mauna Kea and Mauna Loa and playing follow-the-leader among the giant cinder cones in the fantastic crater of Haleakala, the world's largest extinct volcano, with a wild tail-chase down its steep slope to the sea, two miles below its summit. After a series of joint Army-Navy maneuvers we flew out to land aboard the carrier in the roughest seas I have ever seen on a clear day. A gale had blown up giant swells which tossed the *Cabot* around until she appeared to corkscrew. After taking one look at her rolling, pitching deck I could not believe that we would go through with the scheduled landings. But up went the landing signal on the flag hoist and down I spiraled, feeling sure that after I had piled up a heap on the deck, the whole outrageous performance would be called off.

On my first approach Bill Hall waved me off, but on the second time around the deck was still empty and I was first aboard, still scared and hardly believing I had made it safely. The ship was rolling so hard I was afraid my plane would slide over the side, but I was held on the forward elevator, just ahead of the barriers, while the deck crew started to fold my wings. Suddenly the plane handlers disappeared, and I knew from past experience what *that* meant. Once before I had seen the plane handlers vanish as if by magic when an incoming plane had failed to catch a wire, jumping the barriers and smashing down into the parked planes beyond. No matter how busy these men are, they always keep one eye on the incoming planes. When anything goes wrong they are the first ones to spot the trouble, and they can clear the deck in nothing flat. Now I saw them do just that, so that I knew what was coming, even before I could turn my head for a quick look.

The ship's stern had been pitched high into the air

by a huge wave just as an incoming pilot had cut his throttle, so that his plane had been bounced clear over the arresting wires. It was now bearing down on me like a runaway truck. It was too late to do anything but duck. I leaned forward to bury my head between my knees out of harm's way, but I had forgotten to release my shoulder straps. This caused my stomach muscles to tighten up in a violent cramp which was so painful that I hardly noticed the racket the plane behind me made as it hit the barriers. When I finally was able to straighten up and look around I saw Pat Patterson grinning at me from the cockpit of the nosed-up plane in the barrier. He had acted quickly as he saw himself running out of deck and had nosed over into the barriers, thus avoiding a crash which could easily have killed us both. I lost no time in getting out of my plane as soon as the chocks were under the wheels, and watched apprehensively until Bill Hall had brought the rest of his chickens safely back to roost. After that day I never again worried about the Hellcat's ability to land under adverse conditions.

At the completion of this cruise Jim Vredenburgh was detached to become executive officer of the CVE *Marcus Island,* and I succeeded him as air group commander.* His executive officer, Lt. E. E. Wood, was designated commanding officer of the torpedo squadron. Neither of us could believe it at first. Promotions were really coming fast in war time.

* *Editor's Note:* An air group is a carrier's entire complement of planes, which may be composed of one or more squadrons of fighters, dive bombers, and/or torpedo planes.

Task Force 58

BY THE MIDDLE of January there was an under-current of anticipation spreading through the Fleet which reached a peak when an ammunition barge was towed alongside the *Cabot* and the big cranes began to lift huge bombs and torpedoes aboard. Next we began loading stores and taking on fuel oil until the ship had a pronounced list to starboard from the weight of its island structure, indicating that she was loaded to capacity. All conjectures regarding our destination were scattered to the four winds when an officer messenger handed me a bulky sealed packet marked "Commander Air Group Thirty-One—Top Secret." This contained the operations plan for the invasion of the Marshall Islands.

In these detailed operations orders we found that the *Cabot* was to be a part of a task force composed of battleships, cruisers, destroyers, and fast carriers, which excluded the slower and more vulnerable escort carriers, the CVE's. The official designation of this fast carrier task force was Task Force 58. There were several copies of the operations orders which I distributed to the division leaders of both squadrons. As we sat around the ready room studying the various sections of the plan there was a whoop from Patterson.

"Holy Cow!" he yelled. "Look what we're getting for our first combat assignment—the pre-dawn fighter sweep at Kwajalein, over Roi airfield!"

We stared at the operations plan, hardly believing our eyes. Nothing like starting out on the top of the big league! Reading on, we found that the plan called for a surprise assault on Kwajalein, the largest of the Japanese atolls lying to the northwest of their heavily armed bases of Wotje, Jaluit, Mili, and Maloelap, which were the most obvious points for us to attack. Another change from the pattern of previous attacks was that this was not to be another frontal assault of the type which had cost us so heavily at Tarawa in the Gilberts, but a Trojan Horse affair to be launched from within the smoother waters of the protected inner lagoon, using a coordinated land-sea-air attack of the type we had been rehearsing for so many months.

Captain Schoeffel was delighted when he read of our assignment. "We should be proud," he said, "to be on the first team!"

We were proud, all right, but I could not help remembering the repeated warnings we had received regarding the caliber of the Japanese pilots at Roi. No matter how much I tried to throw off the matter as a coincidence, I could not help feeling that Fate had had too big a hand in selecting this particular objective for our introduction to combat. But as the great warships steamed out of Pearl Harbor to a rendezvous off Diamond Head in the bright sunshine, our fears were forgotten. The indecision was over, and at last we were on our way out to fight.

Plowing steadily to the southwest, the huge task force headed for the Gilbert Islands, so that any snooping enemy submarines or reconnaissance planes would be misled as to our ultimate destination. Our course lay to the south of the Gilberts, crossing the Equator at the 180th meridian, so that the calendar got all mixed up at the same time the latitude and longitude directions were reversed. Few of us expected that the traditional ceremonies of "crossing the Line" would be observed in the combat zone, but King Neptune came aboard on schedule with Davy Jones and all his jolly crew, and many a resounding whack echoed across the flight deck as the "Shellbacks" kept the "Pollywogs" properly respectful. That evening many quaint haircuts around the wardroom mess marked the new initiates into the solemn mysteries of the Ancient Order of the Deep and the Royal Order of the Golden Dragon. And that night we memorized the location of the Southern Cross among the strange new constellations above us, to guide us in the event of any sudden need for navigation from our life rafts.

Many times before, in anticipating this situation and wondering how I would react, I had decided that the best way to relax would be simply to put the idea of danger out of my mind, but I had not counted on the repeated reminders in the form of safety drills and battle practice. In the daytime we flew protective patrols around our task group, or towed target sleeves for the ship's anti-aircraft gunners. Those who were not flying took part in various battle problems involving theoretical damage control activities, followed by the inevitable "abandon ship" drill.

Each sunset brought the "darken ship" routine, that naval equivalent of a shore-side blackout which is so vital to survival in enemy waters, where the faintest glimmer of light even from a carelessly exposed cigarette could betray our presence to patrolling enemy submarines and ruin the work of months of planning. With everything battened down the ship was appreciably warmer, in spite of its excellent forced ventilation system. Safety lectures by the air combat intelligence officers stressed the importance of having life jackets and flashlights within reach at all times after dark, and a movie film on survival showed the importance of having sufficient clothing to prevent exposure and being able to get it on in the dark. So it was that no matter how much we tried to ignore the war, it kept saying to us all day long: "I'm still here, see? And you'd better look out, or I'll catch you yet and drag you down!"

This was brought home to me most vividly one night after I had been sleeping soundly for an hour, when the general alarm was sounded without any prior warning. I went sailing out of my bunk before the second *clang* of the gong, as if propelled by a giant spring attached in some manner to the alarm. Grabbing my clothes, I rushed out into the crowded passageway and up into the ready room, stubbing a toe on the way. There we

found that one of the destroyers had reported a sound
contact with a possible submarine, and that we were
taking evasive action rather than using depth charges
which would give our presence away to other subs or
surface vessels. After half an hour of tense waiting the
danger was past, and the bugler gave us "Secure from
General Quarters." I limped back to my bunk and re-
arranged my clothing so that I could hop into it like
a fireman, and from that night on, whenever we were
at sea I slept with my socks on, so that I could jump
into my shoes without a moment's delay. That infernal
general alarm wasn't going to catch me unprepared a
second time.

No matter what alarms the night brought, each sunrise gave us new confidence as we approached our objective without detection by enemy aircraft. After
swinging west below the Gilberts, the task force headed
northwest past the Jap-held islands of Nauru and Kusaie. Still our progress was unopposed. Each day as we
flew our patrol above the force I watched the great
battlewagons and carriers plowing along in perfect formation, each of the task groups in the force maintain-
ing its relative position even on a zigzag course—over
fifty warships in one gigantic team. Whatever the Japs
had waiting for us, it was obvious to anyone who flew
over Task Force 58 that we had more than enough
power to do the job ahead of us.

Still, it was hard to believe that such a huge force
could steam right into the heart of the enemy's defense
system without being spotted. It was too good to be

true. We began to wonder if instead of stalking the Japs we were ourselves being led into a trap. To make sure that no possibilities were overlooked, our task group commander, Rear Admiral A. E. Montgomery, called a conference of group commanders aboard his flagship, one of the larger carriers. I was catapulted for the short flight to the flagship, where it felt strange to land on such a wide flight deck. After the *Cabot*, this carrier was so big that I had to ask for a guide to lead me to the fighter ready room where the conference was to be held. Here I met Lt. Comdr. Johnny Phillips, who was scheduled to lead the first strike on the enemy target.

"Let's all stick together on this strike," he proposed. "Our SBD's will need the most protection, especially during their approach to the pushover point. They'll be diving down-wind, which means they'll dive from east to west, with the prevailing easterly trade winds. They will start their dives from ten thousand feet, or from the cloud base, if there's an overcast. Be sure to warn your pilots to go easy with radio messages, for the southern attack force will be hitting the south end of the atoll at the same time, and they'll be only forty miles away. If they need help they'll call for us, and if we call they're supposed to come running. And don't shoot down any SBD's. Remember that they're about the same size and shape as a Zero, and in poor light you can hardly tell 'em apart."

After discussing every phase of the plan in detail, we flew back to our respective carriers. Back aboard the

Cabot I sat down with Patterson to write out the flight schedule. We split the flights up evenly so that each pilot would fly approximately the same number of hours. I was to lead the pre-dawn fighter sweep with three divisions, and Pat was to lead the second flight, taking off about the time we were due to leave the target.

That night I turned in early, but tossed around a good deal before I dozed off. It was like the old feeling of the night before the big game during school days.

First Action

FINALLY THE NIGHT dragged by without an alarm
or incident, and I turned off my alarm clock before it
rang. The ship was vibrating slightly from the speed we
were making. At early breakfast in the wardroom no-
body seemed very hungry. I ordered the usual hot cakes
with sausages, but they seemed dry and tasteless, even
with twice the amount of syrup.

In the ready room we wrote down our navigation
data, then checked and rechecked it. The surface wind
was about sixteen knots, which would mean a fairly
rough sea in the event of a water landing. I wondered
whether it would be best to advise the pilots to head
for the lagoon if they were hit or to take their chances
in the rougher water outside, where there was less danger of capture. Before I could decide, Al Masters stuck
his head in the door and said casually, "Pilots, man
your planes. Good luck, gang!"

Filing out of the darkened ready room, we groped
our way along the black flight deck to our planes. Mine
was spotted forward, old Number Twenty, and Mul-
vaney, the enlisted plane captain, helped me into my

parachute harness. From the bridge the bull-horn warned us with a "Stand by to start engines! Stand clear of propellers! Start engines!"

I pressed the starter switch, and the engine caught on the first try. Soon I felt more at ease in the darkness as the old familiar roar deepened and the warm smell of the engine enveloped me. My mouth was unaccountably dry, and I took a swig from my canteen while waiting for the ship to turn directly into the wind. Turning on my oxygen, I checked the mask. The cool fresh taste of the pure oxygen was so soothing I left the mask on for several deep breaths.

This was the most critical moment of the entire operation. If the Japs were waiting for us and hit us just now they could ruin us. A few Zeros strafing our crowded flight decks before our planes were launched could start fires which would mark us for their dive bombers and torpedo planes. The next few minutes could bring fiery disaster, if we had been detected. I felt naked and exposed sitting there in the dark in the middle of the flight deck.

Then the ship's whistle boomed once, and the deck tilted sharply as we started a fast turn to starboard, heading into the wind. As soon as we were steadied down on our new course Al Gurney gave me the signal to turn up my engine and waved me ahead as soon as I opened the throttle. The takeoff run along the darkened deck was made more from memory and by sense of touch than by visual reference, for there was no horizon whatever. As soon as I felt the wheels leave the deck I went on instruments until I had a thousand feet of altitude. After that I could breathe easier. Looking down I could make out the running lights of the other planes as they climbed to join me. Soon there were wing lights in the customary positions around me—Nooy on my wing and Wilson leading the second section with Hancock, one of the new pilots, as his wingman. Mulcahy and Scales were leading the other two divisions. Off to the left and right I could see similar processions of lights spiraling upward as planes from the other carriers climbed to their rendezvous. Occasionally a stray light would circle from one group to another, as pilots who had become confused in the dark tried to locate and identify their respective groups.

As the time to take our departure approached I was disturbed to see that my own group was not complete. There were only two planes in one division and three in the other. What had happened to the three missing planes was anybody's guess; I only hoped that they had not gone over the side in taking off, or spun in during an instrument climb. In any event, their absence was a serious detriment to our combat efficiency. But there was no help for it now, for the striking group was departing for the target and we had to escort them in as best we could.

I had planned to concentrate our fighters in one group for tactical support as top cover at twenty thousand feet, ready to convert this altitude into speed for any attacks required at lower altitudes. This plan was disrupted en route to the target when the strike leader gave

me other orders by radio: "There's a cloud layer over
the target at six thousand feet. Take one of your divisions under the clouds at five thousand, put one just
above the clouds, and send the other up to ten thousand."

This was confusing, in view of previous orders to
concentrate our forces. What I did not know was that
a less experienced pilot had assumed the lead when
Johnny Phillips was held on deck with engine trouble;
but orders were orders, and I deployed my forces accordingly, taking the bottom layer for my own division.
The other two divisions, being incomplete, needed the
protection of all the altitude advantage they could get.

As we approached the target the first grey lines of
light in the east began to show above the clouds. Soon
I could make out darker blotches on the dark sea below
us as we passed over the islands on the western tip of
the lagoon. The tail lights of the SBD's below winked
out one by one as we climbed for altitude. As soon as I
could see the outlines of my wingmen's planes I
switched off my formation lights, and they followed suit.
At this time excited voices began coming in over the
radio from pilots of the southern strike group who had
already began their attacks. One voice said very dis-
tinctly, "My plane is afire and I'm going to try to land
in the water."

The northern tip of the atoll, with the islands of Roi
and Namur, was hidden by a cloud layer several hundred feet deep. Skirting this layer to the south, I caught
a glimpse of the lagoon through a hole in the clouds,

and saw enemy fire for the first time; a ship anchored in the lagoon was sending up a bright stream of tracers. The Japs had been alerted, and knew we were attacking in force.

Circling in a left-hand turn around the cloud layer, I let down cautiously to the northeast until I was even with the base of the clouds at about five thousand feet. Here was where the SBD's should be starting their dives. Sure enough, here came a string of eight or ten planes, strung out in bombing approach formation about fifty yards apart, headed down-wind toward the target. I approached them slowly, watching above and around me to make sure that no enemy fighters pounced on them from above. It was a good thing that we had planned to meet at this point, I observed mentally, or I might have missed seeing these planes against the dark background of the ocean below. In the dim light their outlines were hardly distinguishable. I eased in closer to make sure that they were SBD's and not some of our own Hellcats. It was not until I was less than a hundred yards from the nearest plane that I saw the big red discs painted on its dark brown wings—the Rising Sun insignia of Japan. Instead of covering our own SBD's, I had been flying cover for a bunch of *Japanese Zeros!*

The instant that this realization dawned on me I instinctively fired at the nearest Jap plane, which happened to be in about the middle of the procession. The flash of my guns and the brilliance of the tracers momentarily blinded me so that I could see nothing else.

Whether the first shots I fired at an enemy ever struck home or not I will never know, but they really started some fantastic fireworks. Evidently the Jap pilots had not seen us approach, but as soon as my tracers flamed through the middle of their column, the last three or four planes on the end of the string wheeled and fired at me. At the same time the leading Zeros turned to fire at Wilson and Hancock.

What followed was like a dark nightmare. A string of tracers worked toward me and went through my left wing. I banked sharply to the right, almost into another red stream of bullets from a Jap on my right. I yanked the release to drop my belly tank, without first switching over to an internal fuel supply. A moment later my engine sputtered, then quit cold. At first I thought it had been hit, then I remembered the belly tank, and switched to a full tank. Just then Nooy's plane flashed in front of me. There was a Zero on his tail, firing. As the Jap crossed my sights I fired a string of tracers which he seemed to fly into until they went right into his cockpit. He rolled over and disappeared. More tracers streamed past me. I whipped over in a cartwheel turn toward Nooy, who was ready with a similar turn. As I passed in front of Nooy he clipped the Jap off my tail. Three times more we reversed turns, and every time that our tracers came near a Zero, it would whip over in a split-S and disappear. The old "Thach weave" was really working today, just as Boogie Hoffman had told us it would. A few minutes more and we were in the clear with no more Japs pursuing us.

My heart was pounding and my mouth was dry. Pressing my microphone button, I called to the others, "All fighters, rendezvous five miles west of the target at ten thousand feet!"

Heading west with Nooy, I saw a burst of tracers over the lagoon under the edge of the clouds, then the bright orange fire of a flaming plane which lit up the clouds with a garish glare as it plunged toward the lagoon. Was it one of ours or one of theirs? Where were the rest of our pilots? All sorts of doubts and dreads gripped me as we scanned the skies around us for airplanes—friendly or enemy.

Suddenly Nooy called, "Three planes at two o'clock, level!"

These planes were near our rendezvous point, but this time I was taking no chances. Circling wide, I climbed until there was no chance for a surprise, then moved in slowly until I was sure the planes were friendly. They were Hellcats—Scales with two of his wingmen. A few minutes later Wilson climbed up alone and rejoined us. After circling for a few more minutes without seeing any of our other planes, I led the formation in another circuit of the target. Halfway around, Scales opened up on his radio: "Tallyho! Two Zeros at nine o'clock, up!"

Looking in the direction indicated, I saw two planes about three miles north of us, heading west. We were heading east. Turning toward them, I led our group in a climbing approach on the two planes until I was sure of their identity. By this time the light was stronger.

Furthermore, the two planes were well outlined against a background of white clouds, their long, thin fuselages so different from the bulk of our Hellcats that it was easy to identify them nearly a mile away as enemy Zeros. We were closing fast from slightly below at the eight o'clock position. Evidently neither Jap pilot noticed our approach, for they took no evasive action. At a range of about one hundred and fifty yards I opened fire on the rear plane. It rolled out and dived away, smoking. One of the planes behind me followed on its tail. This was Scales, who fired a long burst into the Jap's engine and cockpit until it blew up in midair in front of him.

Meanwhile I turned my guns on the remaining Zero. As I fired I could see my tracers curving ahead into its wing and the incendiaries flashing along its fuselage just ahead of the cockpit. A large section of its left aileron was knocked off and came flying back past me. The plane fell off to the right and started down. Nooy pounced on it like a hawk and followed it down, firing until it burst into bright flames and disappeared through the clouds.

Closing up the formation I led it for another circuit of the target area. There were no other planes in sight, either friendly or enemy. I glanced at my watch, and could hardly believe that it was already past the time we were scheduled to leave the target, but a quick check of my fuel gauges showed me that it was high time to be on our way if we were to get back aboard.

Setting a compass course for the estimated position

of the task force, I carefully checked all my instruments to make sure that my engine had not been hit. There were a couple of bullet holes through the wings which I eyed apprehensively, wondering if there were others through my hydraulic system or oil lines, but apparently there were no hits in vital spots. Glancing around me, I had a sinking feeling to think that of the twelve planes we had launched for our first combat, only six were returning. We had been royally whipped, I felt, in our first brush with the enemy.

Back aboard the carrier, I hurried down to the ready room, where my first questions were about the six missing pilots. My low morale got a great lift when I was informed that four planes from our flight were already aboard, and that only Hancock and Mulcahy were still unaccounted for. The four pilots who got back ahead of us were from the divisions I had assigned as top cover. They had chased one enemy plane into a cloud, but had seen no other activity of any kind, and were resentful at the way "the rest of you guys had all the fun."

"What about Frank Hancock?" I asked Wilson.

"The last time I saw Hancock," he answered, "he was headed for a cloud with a Zero on his tail that was pouring a bushel of tracers into his fuselage. Five or six of them jumped us after you opened fire on that procession, and they really worked us over. We headed for cloud cover, weaving on the way. Hancock got behind on one weave, and they nailed him."

"Did his plane burn? I saw one flamer over the lagoon."

"No, that was a Jap plane. I got him during a weave."

We heard another plane land on the flight deck above us.

"That's a Hellcat! Who is it?" I asked.

"It's Mulcahy!" someone shouted. "Look at his belly tank!"

We all rushed up to see Mulcahy climb out of his plane, wet with perspiration but intact. There were six bullet holes through his plane's belly tank, which he had tried unsuccessfully to release. Other hits had peppered the engine cowling and the after part of the fuselage. He and his wingman had been jumped from above by two Zeros at ten thousand feet. They dived for cloud cover, where they became separated. Finding himself alone Mulcahy started to climb, when five Zeros spotted him and worked him over. Again he escaped in cloud cover, and managed to climb to twenty thousand feet, where he cruised around trying to find some friendly planes to join up on.

"I didn't see any," he said, "so I thought you had all been shot down. Then I saw those five Japs again, cruising around about five thousand feet below me. One of them was straggling a little behind the others, so I made a stern run on him from above and knocked off his left wing. And do you know, his wingmates never even saw him go down!"

"Then what did you do?"

"Then I zoomed back up to twenty thousand feet and trailed them again until I was in good position for another run, but they saw me coming and started for me so I just stayed in my dive and retired under cloud cover. The next time we take off in the dark let's use our bright lights so our wingmen can find us. Boy, that sure was a Group Grope!"

I began to feel much better, now that the final returns began to come in and it was apparent that we had not taken such a beating after all. A few minutes later my spirits soared as a battered Hellcat circled the *Cabot* and we saw from the number on the fuselage that it was Hancock's plane. Even from the flight deck we could see daylight through the 20-mm. cannon holes in his wings and empennage. Unable to lower his flaps or landing gear, Hancock made a water landing and was picked up by a destroyer uninjured.

When Patterson and his gang returned from the second strike they all complained bitterly that they had not been able to find a single enemy plane over the target. "You guys cleaned 'em all out and didn't leave us a thing!" they grumbled.

This was laudable aggressiveness, but nevertheless I called my boys together that night and pointed out to them how lucky we had been that day.

"That luck won't last," I told them, "unless we learn to stick together and stop breaking formation to chase single planes down after they have been hit. A Jap Zero has no armor, and once you put a string of fifty-caliber slugs through the pilot or engine you don't have to follow it down until it blows up in your face. The object is to do as much damage as you can to the enemy and still come home with a whole skin. We'd also like to have the airplanes back, too. So don't take a chance unless the results to be gained justify the risk, and you'll live longer. Also I'd like to remind you that we haven't had a single operational casualty in the Pacific area. If you can just keep that up you'll set a record that you'll be just as proud of as your combat score. Remember that the extra flight pay you get is because military flying is dangerous, and that an operational casualty just saves Japanese ammunition."

Afterward I called Mulcahy to my room and lectured him privately about the virtues of knowing when to fight and when to run away, pointing out that we needed every airplane and that at the rate we were going we'd be out of business in two weeks unless we could get replacements. After reminding him that only fools and Irishmen rush into a brawl at odds of five to one, I recommended him for the Navy Cross for being so careless.

Invasion of the Marshalls

THAT EVENING after our first day of action we had plenty to be thankful for aboard the *Cabot*. We had no casualties. Not one ship in our task force had been hit, due to the complete surprise we had effected. All enemy air opposition had been wiped out, not only at Kwajalein but at the other enemy bases on nearby islands as well.

A message from our fleet commander, Admiral Spruance, was posted on our ready room bulletin board:

PLEASE EXPRESS TO THE PILOTS OF YOUR TASK GROUP MY APPRECIATION OF THE SPLENDID JOB THEY DID IN TAKING OUT THE ENEMY AIR OPPOSITION AT ROI. A STUDY OF THE PHOTOGRAPHS THEY TOOK OF ROI AND NAMUR SHOWS AN AUSPICIOUS OPENING OF THIS OPERATION.

In the operational data chalked on the blackboard was the following information:

NEAREST LAND	BEARING	DISTANCE
Jaluit (Jap)	065°	225 Miles
Kwajalein (Jap)	011°	315 Miles

Underneath this data some wag had chalked the following comment: "Note: A change in ownership will soon be made."

These were gay words so early in the game, for there was still the possibility of an enemy counter-attack. Our ship was in the westernmost part of the task force, which meant that if the Japs threw a carrier strike at us to break up the invasion, we would probably be the first to make contact. As I stretched out on my bunk and switched off the light I hoped fervently that it would not be a surface engagement at night, but that it would occur in daylight, where we would have a chance to get in on the action instead of sitting helplessly by as a spectator while the surface batteries exchanged broadsides.

I do not recall going to sleep before I was jolted wide awake by the harsh clang of the general alarm gong over the ship's loudspeaker system. Within seconds I was dressed and on my way up to the ready room. Here I saw by the clock that I had been asleep several hours.

Stepping across the passageway into Air Plot, I asked Lt. Comdr. Al Masters what had caused the alarm. "What is it, Al, an air or a submarine contact?"

"Neither," he replied grimly. "This is a *surface* contact—visual. Take a squint outside, off the starboard quarter. And put your tin hat on first."

Grabbing my steel helmet, I groped my way through the darkened light-lock to the starboard catwalk. What I saw gave me cold chills, for a powerful searchlight was sweeping the seas, its bright white beam barely above our task group, from a source just over the horizon. Someone was looking for a target, and we were doing our best to keep out of the spotlight by heading at top speed away from its source.

As we watched we saw the flash of gunfire at the base of the searchlight beam, so close that we could see the tracers of medium-caliber shells as they cut red arcs through the black night. Seconds later the flashes of the exploding shells could be seen, and in a few moments a red glare lit up the sky. Here was our surface engagement, all too soon.

Over the ship's loudspeaker system an officer on the bridge began describing the scene for the benefit of the ship's personnel whose battle stations were below decks. This included the majority of the fifteen hundred souls aboard, for only a small proportion of the crew of any big warship ever sees what goes on in a battle; most of the crew is sealed behind several water-tight compartments.

"There's some kind of surface action going on to the north of us," said the announcer, gulping audibly into the microphone. "We can't tell what it is just yet, but some ship is shelling a surface target. We don't know whether it's ours or theirs. There's a searchlight sweeping around, but it's too high to pick us up, I think. Now they're firing again—it looks like five-inch guns. They give off quite a flash, like lightning beyond the horizon. There, they've hit something, and it's burning—quite a big fire. Well, they're firing to the east, so they can't be firing at us. Now they're firing to the west. All hands,

put on your flash-proof clothing. All personnel whose
battle stations are not topside, clear the flight deck!"

Back I ducked into the ready room, where my pilots
sat with tense faces, while the announcer continued:
"Now there are fires on both sides of the searchlight.
That must be quite a *melee* going on up there. Now the
firing has stopped and the flashlight—I mean searchlight
—is looking for more targets. Well, I think we're getting
almost out of range, I hope!"

We began to relax, until the announcer came on again
a few minutes later with a new threat to our peace of
mind: "We've got a bogey reported, either one plane
or a small group of planes, heading in from the west.
There will be no firing by the anti-aircraft batteries
unless the task group commander gives the order by
signal. We still hope we haven't been located. The fires
up north are still burning, but the firing has stopped
and the searchlight is out. We're out of range now,
anyway, as far as surface shelling is concerned. The
bogey is now reported overhead, but it's pretty high
and doesn't appear to be changing course. Maybe they
won't spot us."

Everyone waited tensely for the next report, which
came a few minutes later: "The bogey apparently
missed us, as it is now heading east toward Wotje or
Mili. Secure from General Quarters."

We stared at each other unbelievingly. The crisis had
passed, and the surface action for which we had braced
ourselves was no longer a threat. We hung around the
wardroom for a while just to make sure, but everything

was so quiet and normal that we were soon back in our bunks. Once again I dropped off to sleep and slept soundly until the squadron duty officer called me as scheduled, three hours before sunrise, for the dawn patrol.

The reason for such early rising was that a combat air patrol had to be in the air over each task group in time to protect it from any attack by enemy aircraft just before sunrise, which is when we would be most vulnerable to a surprise attack. Our anti-submarine patrols were launched at the same time. These patrols were relieved on station every four or five hours, so that a continuous aerial patrol guarded the ship from dawn to dusk.

At this time of the year, January 30, sunrise was at 0717. Reveille for the ship's Air Department, including the pilots on the first flight, was at 0345. Breakfast was at 0400, which gave the pilots half an hour to get to the ready room, where they were mustered one hour before manning the planes. This hour was spent in working out the navigation problem for the flight, copying down the day's recognition signals and other flight data, and checking personal equipment such as flashlights, pneumatic life jackets, and the emergency landing equipment in our parachute back packs. By the time all engines were started and warmed up it would be six o'clock, and another half hour before all planes had been catapulted, had made their rendezvous, and had climbed to the assigned altitude. By that time the sun's first rays would be tinting the tops of the taller thunderheads, although sunrise at sea-level was still almost an hour away.

A four- or five-hour patrol in a fighter is no picnic, for you cannot move around and must remain strapped in your seat in the heat at low altitudes in the tropics, or chilled to the bone at the higher altitudes. You circle the task group hour after hour, changing from a right turn to a left turn every hour to break the monotony. Unless enemy planes are in the vicinity it is very dull, and it is a great relief to be able to land and stretch out cramped legs and sore muscles. Occasionally a flight may be unavoidably prolonged to as many as a total of six hours, in which case the pilot is usually very sore indeed. After such flights we used to issue each pilot a "sympathy chit," which bore the following legend:

SIX-HOUR PATROL

SYMPATHY CHIT

This entitles you to a good cry on the shoulder of the Flight Officer at *your* convenience.

Signed: I. M. Sorry,
SQUADRON MORALE OFFICER.

Not one of our anti-submarine or combat air patrols produced a single enemy contact during the entire Marshalls invasion. Our pilots were bored stiff and stiff as boards before it was half completed, except when they were assigned close air-support missions over the target. These latter flights were bombing or strafing missions, usually not more than a two- or three-hour flight. A target coordinator designated specific ground targets such as enemy pillboxes or machine-gun nests for our pilots to hit. My boys enjoyed these assignments because it gave them a chance to see how the invasion was going as well as to fire their guns and drop bombs. I tried to assign all flights so that each pilot gained experience in all types of assignment. I also led each new type of flight, such as the first night catapult shot, the first takeoff with thousand-pound bombs plus full belly tanks, or the first pre-dawn fighter sweep, before I assigned any other pilot to make such a flight.

At breakfast that morning I learned what had sent us to battle stations during the preceding night. One of our picket destroyers, sent out ahead of the task group to search for enemy surface patrols, had steamed right into the middle of a convoy of half a dozen Japanese cargo ships which were fleeing ahead of our invasion. Our destroyer had swept its searchlight back and forth a few times to make sure of its targets, and had then blasted away with its five-inch guns until the entire convoy was ablaze or sinking.

The plane which had crossed in the dark had evidently been evacuating enemy personnel from one of the island bases, for it had paid no attention to us as it passed overhead. In the daylight we could laugh at our fears of the night before, but there were other nights to come.

Our dawn patrol that day proved to be unproductive, as were all of our subsequent patrols during the

Marshalls invasion. Although we were in enemy territory, our only contact with the enemy was when we
bombed or strafed his installations on Roi and Namur
or the adjacent small islands. This brought up the question of what constituted a combat mission, as far as our
pilots were concerned. We decided that the only fair
way to designate such a mission was whether or not it
resulted in damage either to the enemy or to ourselves.
Thus a combat air patrol which produced no enemy
contact was not considered a combat mission, while a
bombing or strafing flight which destroyed enemy installations or which resulted in anti-aircraft damage
to our planes was considered a combat mission, as far
as the individual pilot's record was concerned.

It was necessary to make such a decision in order to
keep our eager pilots in line. Those who did not encounter enemy planes during routine patrol flights
howled to high heaven when their more fortunate
friends were able to chase a bogey or two during later
flights. They felt that there were simply not enough
enemy planes to go around, and that those who had
shot down any Japanese aircraft should be retired to
a bench on the sidelines until the rest of the team had
a chance to score.

This brought up another touchy question which I had
not anticipated—that of individual credit for enemy
airplanes destroyed. Suppose two or more pilots fired
on the same Japanese airplane, as several of us had in
our first encounter. Who would get credit for the kill:
the pilot who scored the first hit, the pilot who did the

most damage, or the pilot who finally set the enemy plane afire or blew it up? In many cases an entire division of fighters had been known to make repeated runs on an enemy bomber or patrol plane before knocking it out. Other squadrons, I knew, frequently split the credit, assigning each pilot involved in the action an equal share, such as one-half, one-fourth, or even one-eighth or one-twelfth. This I considered a very unsatisfactory system, for I had known cases where pilots had returned from previous tours of combat duty with only fractions of enemy planes to their credit after several combat missions. A former student of mine had reported to me rather sheepishly that although his four-plane division had shot down several Japanese bombers, his official score of enemy planes destroyed was one and five-eighths.

"That is a silly system," I told my pilots. "We will give credit where credit is due, as far as possible, using eye-witness testimony and camera-gun films for damage assessment. You always know among yourselves who really deserves the credit. Each division will decide who gets credit for individual kills, and we won't bother about any fractions. What do you think about it?"

They all liked the idea, and it worked very satisfactorily. The important thing was that each man got credit for what he had contributed, even though the reward was only a pat on the back or a sincere "well done" from the squadron commander or the ship's captain. My pilots didn't seem to mind about the long delay between the recommendation and the actual presentation of a decoration; the main thing was that someone recognized their contribution and told them about it.

They were also very touchy about newspaper or magazine publicity. One of my wingmen received an airmailed copy of a weekly news magazine, shortly after our first action, which described the whole Marshalls invasion as a pushover, saying that "no aerial opposition was encountered over the target."

Frank Hancock, whose plane had been so thoroughly riddled over Roi, snorted when he read this item.

"Maybe they were ghost planes," he said, "but they had red spots on their wings and they were sure throwin' a lot of hot lead around mighty careless!"

Yankee Audacity

AFTER OUR carrier-based planes had bombed the Japanese installations on Roi and Namur for a couple of days the islands began to look a bit moth-eaten. The hangars were charred skeletons. Burnt-out airplane fuselages littered the airfield like crushed grasshoppers. The runways were scarred and pitted with bomb craters until they looked like a view of the moon through an observatory telescope.

Then we circled above the lagoon while our battleships and cruisers steamed up in a stately procession to within a few miles of the coral reef just off shore, firing their heavy batteries while their observation planes spotted each salvo and reported the results. The big ships steamed up and down north of the reef, firing to starboard as they headed east and to port after they reversed their course and headed west. When they completed their bombardment the two target islands looked as if they had been struck by a gigantic hailstorm followed by a plague of locusts. Trees and buildings had been leveled. The outlines of the airfield's runways could barely be discerned. Even from the air the de-

structive power of a naval bombardment was appall-
ingly evident. From that day on, the aviators who had
seen the big battlewagons pulverize some of the enemy's
strongest defensive positions would be among their
staunchest supporters.

The most fascinating aerial view of the invasion was
the launching of the first amphibious attack wave on
D-Day, when the landing craft swarmed around their
parent ships in concentric circles like so many water
bugs, then suddenly streaked in parallel white lines for
the beach in a weird geometric pattern of coordinated
striking power. What we saw there at Kwajalein would
be repeated many times on the road to Tokyo, but this
was the battle baptism of a new system based on all the
knowledge earned so dearly at Tarawa. Not long afterward our tanks drove across the battered airfield, and
a few days later Kwajalein was ours.

It was only a week after our first carrier strike that
we cruised east from Kwajalein, glad to get a relief for
a while from the monotonous routine of unproductive
patrols. Everyone assumed that we were heading back
to Pearl Harbor to refuel and replenish our depleted
bomb and ammunition supplies, but to our surprise we
headed southeast instead. The scuttlebutt was that we
were going to a new anchorage in one of the captured
Marshall Islands lagoons, and this actually proved to be
the case.

While we had been hitting Kwajalein, other task
groups of our force had been pounding the remaining
Marshall Islands strongholds of the Japs, some of which

were possibly more strongly fortified than even **Tarawa**, in the expectation that they would be next on our schedule after the invasion of the Gilbert Islands. These island fortresses southeast of Kwajalein included Jaluit, Mili, Wotje, and Maloelap with its big airfield on the island of Taroa. Any one of these four islands, all of which had airfields, could easily have been as tough an assault problem as Tarawa had been. Almost in their center was another large atoll whose island rim was too low and narrow for adequate defense installations. It had not been fortified by the Japanese, so that our troops were able to occupy it with little or no resistance.

This was Majuro Atoll, whose deep lagoon with only one narrow entrance formed an ideal harbor where a large fleet could anchor without fear of submarine attack. Through this passage our ships carefully nosed their way in single file until our entire task group was anchored inside the smooth waters of the lagoon. As ship after ship cruised slowly up to head into the easterly trade wind and drop its anchor as nonchalantly as if in Chesapeake Bay or Pearl Harbor, our amazement at the audacity of our admirals increased. Then another task group arrived, to be followed by still another, with *Iowa*-class battleships anchored only a few hundred yards from *Essex*-class carriers, until most of the ships of Task Force 58 lay grouped together like so many sitting ducks, right in the middle of the hottest hornets' nest of enemy air bases east of Truk.

At first we thought there would at least be room to maneuver inside the lagoon in the event of an enemy air attack, but soon it was obvious that even the defense of mobility would no longer be available to us.

"What on earth are they thinking of?" asked one of the ship's officers incredulously. "We haven't even got an airstrip here to launch fighters if we're attacked!"

"Maybe they intend to catapult us while we're at anchor!" suggested one pilot facetiously.

Our catapult officer got out his slide rule and made a few quick calculations. "I think it could be done in a pinch," he announced. "We've got a twelve-to-fifteen-knot wind here, and we might be able to get away with it."

Several pilots howled at the very idea. "That's what *you* think!" cried one. "*You* don't have to *fly* the airplane! How would *you* like to be shot off the deck with your own slingshot?"

"When the Japs find us, I'd rather be shot off than to sit here and take it with the ship at anchor," retorted the catapult officer.

This discussion was cut short by the sound of the general alarm gong clanging away on a nearby ship. Over our bull-horn the officer of the deck asked the reason, and back came the answer: "Large bogey coming in from the south at about twenty thousand feet!"

With that announcement our own general alarm went into action, joining its brazen clangor to the general uproar. Ducking into the ready room, I pulled on my parachute harness and hurried up to the flight deck. The nearest plane was a Hellcat sitting on the catapult. Climbing into the cockpit, I called to the squadron

duty officer: "Check with Air Plot and keep me posted
on the bearing, distance, and altitude of the bogey!"

Overhead the noonday sun beat down upon me as I
sat in the cockpit, and in a few moments I was sweating
it out as I waited for the signal to go. Checking the engine at full power, I pushed the propeller governing
control as far forward as I could get it; as long as I had
to be the guinea pig in such an unrehearsed experiment
I wanted all the RPM I could get.

Without the usual gale across the flight deck it grew
hotter and hotter until I began to feel that even getting
dunked in the lagoon would be a welcome relief. Then
a blast from the yodler on the bridge notified us to
throttle our engines down so that we could hear an
announcement over the ship's bull-horn: "Stop all engines!"

As I cut my switches the S.D.O. climbed up on the
wing and gave me the reason: "The bogey was friendly
—probably Army bombers on the way north from Tarawa to hit Eniwetok."

The alert was over, and we secured from battle stations. In spite of our misgivings, that was the only time
we went to General Quarters in Majuro lagoon. Later
on we were to see aircraft catapulted successfully from
ships anchored all around us, until we began to take it
as a matter of course. It was like the old story of Colum-
bus showing how to stand an egg on end: once we had
seen it done, there was no trick to it at all.

The longer our task force sat unmolested in Majuro
lagoon the more we marvelled that the Japs were not

hitting night and day with everything they had. But if it was even partly bluff, it worked. Our Navy's challenge to the Japanese, one of the most audacious in the history of naval warfare, was never accepted. Daily our aerial patrols raked the enemy's nearby island airfields, keeping the runways out of commission and bombing every building large enough to hide even part of an airplane. Our carrier-based air arm had walked right into the heart of the enemy's land-based air force, smashing it down and keeping it impotent. The island airfields which had once been described as "unsinkable aircraft carriers" now proved to be death-traps for their by-passed garrisons.

Gradually it became apparent to all of us that the invasion of the Marshalls was approaching completion as far as the Navy was concerned. We had two new fleet anchorages bigger than a dozen Pearl Harbors in the spacious lagoons of Kwajalein and Majuro. Within a few days our Seabees had new coral airstrips available for our Corsairs and Liberators to take over the job of keeping the Japs pinned down on their by-passed island bases. We no longer had to cruise all the way back to Pearl Harbor to rearm and for replacements. Again we began to wonder where we were headed next.

"This time it's Rabaul for sure," ventured one pilot.

"No, I bet we hit Eniwetok," said another.

"Don't be silly! That's too close to Truk! They'd blow us out of the water."

"Well, the next closest island is Wake, and we've got enough power here to do the job."

Photographs

The author in "Old Faithful," his favorite Grumman Hellcat (F6F). This is the plane he first flew into combat. Note the "Flying Meataxe" insignia.

A division of four Grumman Hellcats (F6F) flying in two-plane sections. The broken coastline may be glimpsed through the cloud formations.

The author's Grumman Wildcat (F4F-3) after chopping down half a dozen Florida pine trees in a dead-stick landing after a midair collision. [See Chapter Two.]

The original pilots of Fighting Squadron 31.
Left to right, front row: Winston, Patterson, Mencin, Kona, Jemison. Second row: Wilson, Hawkins, Nooy, Galt, Carr. Third row: Scales, Wirth, Hedrick, Zimmerman, Charity. Fourth row: Bowie, Hayde, Anderson, Loomis.

The squadron after being doubled. Left to right, standing: Winston, Patterson, Conant, Reiger, Mulcahy, Froelick, Mencin, Wilson, Galt, Wirth, Anderson. Kneeling: Dietrich, Godsey, Osborne, Duggins, Jemison, Turner, Carr, Nooy, Hawkins, Hayde, Andrews. Sitting: Hancock, Edwards, Elezian, Whitworth, Pacosa, Kona, Hedrick, Zimmerman, Bowie, Scales.

Part of Task Force 58 in Majuro lagoon less than a week after its capture. The *Cabot* is on the extreme left. Another CVL, the *Monterey*, is in foreground. [See Chapter Ten.]

A Jap plane splashes during the Marianas "Turkey Shoot," while the *Cabot's* gunners watch. The black dot under the shell bursts is the author's plane. [See Chapter Seventeen.]

The end of the trail. The vanguard of the Third Fleet steams into Tokyo Bay for the occupation of Japan, after nearly four years of war.

It was soon obvious that we were up to no good, for the tankers and ammunition barges were alongside, refueling and rearming the *Cabot* until she took on the list to starboard which we knew meant business was at hand again.

Nearly a week had passed since we had dropped our hook in Majuro's lagoon, when Captain Schoeffel sent for me.

"I want you to go over to the flagship with me," he said, "to discuss a little training operation that's coming up soon."

The captain's gig was our Number One motor-whale-boat with a canvas canopy over the forward half to keep out the spray. We bounced across the waves kicked up by the steady trade wind for nearly an hour before we reached the *Essex*-class carrier which was the flagship of our task group.

Aboard the flagship we were greeted by Admiral Montgomery's Chief of Staff, Captain Jack Moss. He and Captain Schoeffel had evidently discussed the forthcoming operation in considerable detail, as they went right into the subject of ship dispositions. Pointing to a chart on the bulkhead behind me, Captain Moss outlined the situation to Captain Schoeffel.

"We will come in from the northeast, while the other task groups hit from the center and left flank."

Glancing back over my shoulder at the chart, I saw that Captain Moss was pointing to a large-scale reproduction of an atoll entirely unfamiliar to me.

"By the way, Winston doesn't know our destination

as yet," said Captain Schoeffel. Then he added casually, "We are going to hit Truk."

All I could do was gulp and stare unbelievingly at the cluster of islands on the chart. The two captains went on discussing the Japanese fortifications as though we were planning a ship's picnic instead of an assault on the enemy's most formidable island fortress.

"It will be a two-day strike," Captain Schoeffel continued. "While we hit Truk, an expeditionary task group will invade Eniwetok. We had hoped to catch a large part of the Japanese fleet in Truk lagoon, but from reconnaissance photos it looks as though we'll be disappointed."

Thank Heaven, I thought, *we won't have to take on the whole Japanese Fleet at the same time we hit Truk!*

Strike on Truk

AS SOON AS we were back on the *Cabot* I sat down
with a copy of the operations plan and studied it carefully. From the previous comments I had heard from
various pilots it was obvious that some fast work was
necessary to prevent them from being mentally handi-
capped by Truk's reputation for impregnability to the
point where they would be beaten before the fighting
ever started. What we were up against was more a fear
of the unknown rather than a specific fear of a known
quantity. If I could only deflate the build-up which my
pilots had given Truk in their own minds, they would
go into action with confidence instead of dread and un-
certainty.

By this time I knew that most of our pilots feared
capture more than death or injury. They would take
far greater chances over or near their own ships than
over enemy bases where the chances of rescue were
slim. Another great worry was that of being left behind
after a water landing to die by the slow torture of thirst
and starvation. Bullet-proof armor and self-sealing fuel
tanks had been so successful that the average pilot

hardly considered the possibility of being killed or injured even if he were shot down.

From reading the details of the prospective Truk attack it was evident that in this operation the fear of capture would be particularly strong. All of the objectives at Truk were well inside the surrounding coral reef. Prevailing winds and currents were toward Truk and other Japanese-held islands. The plan of retiring after the second day's operations made it clear that any castaway adrift after the retirement would probably end up shortly either as a prisoner or a corpse.

By anticipating these fears, it was possible to neutralize them before they could start any deterioration of pilot morale. Calling the air group together for a conference before the identity of the objective was announced, I casually informed them that we were about to depart for a short period of operations against a nearby Japanese island base. (Most pilots envisioned Eniwetok, Kusaie, or Wake.) I then told them that we had recent reconnaissance photos of the objective which indicated that its strength was not nearly as formidable as had previously been estimated, and that our attacking air strength would be several times as large as the enemy's defending force. When this information had been received with apparent satisfaction, I quietly announced that the objective was Truk.

Before the initial shock of surprise could sink in, I outlined the rough details of the operations plan on large-scale charts of the objective, stressing our disappointment at finding such a weakened garrison and so few surface targets, due to the simultaneous drives on Rabaul and Paramushiro. In this first discussion of the problem I stressed all our advantages and did not mention enemy advantages unless specific questions brought them to light, in which case I minimized them as much as was truthfully possible. I went into the rescue facilities in great detail, emphasizing the large number of airplanes, submarines, and surface vessels available. One master stroke in the operations order was of great assistance in allaying pilots' fears of capture. This order urged pilots to make every effort to land outside of the lagoon if forced down, so that fewer rescuing seaplanes would be brought under enemy shore-based gunfire. The mere possibility of being picked up inside of Truk lagoon by a friendly seaplane had never occurred to any pilot, and the announcement of such unexpected rescue facilities relaxed the last tense faces in the ready room.

Where the unknown had been terrifying, it was now the old story of familiarity breeding contempt. The more the pilots studied the installations on Truk, the greater their confidence grew, until they were actually more relaxed than they had been before the previous action over Roi and Namur. Another result which I had not anticipated was that in giving this sales talk to the air group I had also convinced myself that Truk was highly overrated and due for an unpleasant surprise, with a consequent rise in my own confidence.

Our air group's assignment in the first day's strikes promised to be very interesting, for this time we were assigned the combat air patrols over our task group at a time when large-scale retaliatory attacks by the enemy could be expected. In addition to these patrols our torpedo squadron was assigned several airfield targets and shipping strikes. The *Essex*-class carriers with their larger fighting squadrons were to handle the preliminary fighter sweeps, but our own fighting squadron was assigned to plant some 1000-pound bombs with delayed action fuses on the enemy's bomber runways.

One disconcerting feature of the approach and final high-speed run-in to the target was that there would be moonlight to aid any enemy bombers that might pick us up. A bomber's moon, we recalled, had given the task force a bad night during the invasion of the Gilbert Islands.

However, the approach was made undetected, and complete surprise was achieved at the target. The Japanese fighter pilots were confused and overwhelmed by the aggressive Hellcat pilots who strafed them on the ground and blasted them out of the air. Over two hundred Jap planes were destroyed, of which one hundred and twenty-seven were shot down in aerial combat. All air opposition over the target was soon cleaned out.

Our combat air patrols over the task group were unproductive, for no enemy planes succeeded in following our pilots back. There were enough false alarms, nevertheless, to make our morning sufficiently exciting. These were usually small groups or single planes of our own forces straggling back from the target. Each of these had to be investigated to make sure that it was friendly, and each interception was made as though the planes in question were enemy.

On one patrol I was catapulted with a loose cockpit latch which fell out and dropped into the bottom of the cockpit out of reach. Not wishing to let this keep me out of the fighting, I closed the cockpit canopy as tightly as I could and used a radio jack cord to hold it in place. This makeshift arrangement worked satisfactorily until my division went out on a vector at high speed to investigate a reported bogey. These incoming planes were at low altitude, so that in letting down to their level we picked up over three hundred knots.

This airspeed was too much for my defective canopy, which let go with a bang. Luckily it blew outward instead of inward, or it could easily have knocked me out. As it was, it hit me over the top of the head with a jolt that left my ears ringing. Easing out of the dive, I found that the cockpit canopy was jammed in such a manner that I could not budge it, either to roll it back or jettison it by means of the emergency release. In the event of a forced landing I would be pinned in the cockpit just as I had been after that midair collision at Jacksonville.

Once again I had the same frustrated, panicky feeling of being trapped, but this time I did not have a dead engine. Calling my wingmen by radio, I notified them of my predicament and headed back for the task group. The canopy was bent down and back in such a manner that it was wedged behind the back of my neck. This kept my head much lower than usual, so that I was barely able to see over the edge of the cockpit.

Back over the *Cabot* I outlined the situation by radio and made a trial run before attempting to land. This was a worthwhile precaution, for I could barely see the signal officer, and could not see the flight deck at all. After notifying the ship that I could not see the deck from approach position I requested permission to try to land on one of the bigger carriers.

After a short pause the answer came back: "Permission granted. Try Blank Base." This was the U.S.S. *Essex*, which was also in our task group. After a preliminary circuit to look the situation over, I found that by cocking my plane up on one wing in a forward slip I could see the L.S.O. He gave me a cut in spite of my sloppy approach, so that all I had to do was sit back and hold everything until I felt the arresting gear take hold, landing more from memory than by visual reference to the flight deck. This worked fine on a flight deck as big as that of the *Essex*, and in a few moments I was spotted on the elevator and lowered to the cavernous hangar deck, where the bent canopy was cut off from behind my neck by a couple of mechanics. Half an hour later I was catapulted to make the short flight back to the *Cabot, sans* canopy, where the damage was soon repaired.

We could always count on our maintenance division on the *Cabot* to patch up our planes in record time. The sparkplug of this outfit was a tireless reserve lieutenant named "Red" Sherman, whose energy and foresight saved many an airplane which would otherwise have been scrapped for salvage. His crew of enlisted plane captains took such personal pride in keeping our Hellcats in shape that I had their names stenciled on the planes to which they were assigned. This made it a point of pride with each man to keep his particular airplane in tip-top shape, with the result that the *Cabot* lost fewer planes from operational causes than any other CVL in the fleet.

BY NIGHTFALL over a score of enemy ships had been sunk, including a cruiser and two smaller warships caught by our surface forces after they had tried to run for safety through Truk's north pass. Two of my Avenger pilots had blasted an airfield full of parked twin-engined Bettys with incendiary bombs, destroying twelve of the enemy's best long-range torpedo-bombers, while their squadron commander, Lt. Wood, had sunk a ten-thousand-ton cargo ship with one salvo of five-hundred-pounders.

That night we retired at high speed to the northeast, hoping that the delayed action bombs which we had left on Truk's airfields would discourage any enemy planes from taking off to follow us. All was quiet until the moon rose, when bogies were reported approaching from the west. This time no one was surprised when the bugle sounded "General Quarters" and the loudspeaker blared: "All hands, man your battle stations! Set condition Able!" For some reason this was more comforting than the jarring clang of the general alarm which always came as a shock even when it was tested each morning at breakfast time.

A short time later a line of parachute flares appeared a few miles off our port beam. We watched these ghostly lights apprehensively as they drifted slowly down, silhouetting our ships for the torpedo attack which we knew would begin at any moment.

Then the announcer on the bridge spoke up: "All pilots clear the flight deck! Bogies are closing only a few miles off our starboard quarter!"

Down in the ready room just below the flight deck our pilots sat tensely waiting for the enemy to strike, unable to do anything but sit there and take it without lifting an arm in self defense. They were too quiet; it was easy to see that their morale was at a low ebb. I recalled that by minimizing their normal fears prior to the assault on Truk we had been able to eliminate most of their worries, and decided to try it again.

"I'm glad we're on a CVL," I announced as unconcernedly as I could manage to appear. "Those Nips are probably trying to figure out which is the flagship among the big carriers. We've got over eighty ships out here, so that the odds against our being hit are pretty good. I don't see any sense in keeping all of you up here and missing out on a good night's sleep when you have to fly tomorrow. You might just as well go on back to your bunks and relax, as long as you remain dressed. Get as much rest as you can. If we need you the duty officer will pass the word."

The pilots looked at each other for a moment in surprise, then filed out of the ready room to go to their own rooms. My purpose in this move was not only to give them more rest, but also to get them dispersed so that we would not have all our eggs in one basket in case a lucky hit set off the 40-mm. ammunition stowed next to the ready room.

Even in their bunks the pilots could still hear what was being announced over the loudspeaker system. "The bogies are now passing overhead," said the announcer. "We can hear their engines. The Task Group is still withholding its fire to keep from giving the enemy a better target. There are only a few planes, probably ferried in to Truk from other bases right after we left the target."

There was a short pause. "The carrier next to us has just announced that she has been torpedoed," he continued in a casual voice. "It is the *Intrepid*. She is still making her normal speed. These Jap torpedoes must not be big enough to sink a modern carrier."

After a longer pause he continued. "The enemy planes are now retiring to the westward. Apparently they have dropped all their torpedoes. Secure from General Quarters."

This sudden end to the attack was almost an anticlimax. We waited expectantly, never doubting that the Japs would send out several successive waves to hit us, but there were no further alarms that night, and my pilots got an unexpected good night's sleep.

At breakfast we learned that the *Cabot* had been detailed to escort the torpedoed *Intrepid* back to Majuro, which meant that all our scheduled strikes on Truk for that day were cancelled. This brought considerable grumbling from those pilots who had been assigned to the unproductive combat air patrols the day before without having a chance to see what Truk looked like. Their disappointment was still more bitter to learn that they had missed out on an even more historic operation. The rest of the task force, finding no worthwhile shipping targets left in Truk's lagoon after noon of the second day, called off the remaining scheduled flights and steamed northwest for a strike on the Marianas. En route they were detected by enemy search planes and fought their way in under almost continuous attack by enemy bombers and torpedo planes—the first time a carrier task force had run into land-based aerial operation before launching its strikes. Guam, Saipan, and Tinian were hit by our forces for the first time, and the task force retired without damage after shooting down over fifty planes and destroying half again as many on the ground, with a loss of only four U.S. planes. This was fantastic success for such an inauspicious beginning; obviously the Japanese had been caught completely off guard.

The enemy had been stung severely where it would hurt the most, and in a telling manner that was at least partial repayment in kind for his sneak carrier assault on Pearl Harbor.

Shortly afterward a message was received from Admiral Nimitz congratulating all who participated in the

Truk strike. Tremendous damage was inflicted on the enemy. He regretted that more enemy combatant ships were not present to meet destruction. "The Navy and the country are proud of you."

Task Force 58 lost nineteen airplanes in the strike on Truk, but so large a percentage of the pilots and crews were picked up that we were all amazed, especially at some of the seaplane rescues of pilots downed inside the lagoon. It was evident that the Navy's rescue policy was bearing fruit, for the more confidence our pilots had in being picked up, the more they were willing to risk hitting the enemy at close range.

Running the Gantlet

AFTER REFUELLING at Majuro the *Cabot* escorted the *Intrepid* back to Pearl Harbor for repairs. Here we spent nearly two weeks ashore, using airplanes at Kaneohe to keep in practice. This gave us a chance to brush up on our bombing and gunnery and to relax a bit. First we threw an air group party at the officers' club, then settled down to fishing trips or surf swimming at Makapuu Beach, where big rollers provided the best body-surfing on the island of Oahu. My pilots enjoyed this type of surf-riding better than the surf-boards at Waikiki Beach, where only the Hawaiians seemed to be able to master the knack of riding the big native surf-boards.

About the middle of March we received our next operations orders from CINCPAC's headquarters. Our next strike was to be deep into enemy-controlled waters. It called for a cruise of nearly four thousand miles to the Palau Islands by way of Majuro, running the gantlet of Japanese island bases between Truk and New Guinea. The purpose of the operation was to smash enemy shipping and to mine the land locked harbor of

Palau, so that the Japanese would be unable to use its facilities for staging in reinforcements to their bases on New Guinea, which were scheduled to be invaded shortly by an amphibious operation at Hollandia, about half way along the north coast of the big island.

The cruise from Pearl Harbor to Palau required nearly two weeks, and as we steamed steadily westward without meeting aerial opposition from any of the island bases along our route, the probability of a surface engagement increased with each mile of our progress into the enemy's back yard. The farther we went the more it looked like a trap. Palau itself was only about three hours by air from the dozen enemy airfields on Mindanao in the Philippine Islands—considerably west of Tokyo's longitude. One rear admiral in charge of a task group developed a sick headache just from thinking about it.

"If the Japs play this right," he was quoted as saying, "they've got us just where they want us."

Such estimates of the situation did not improve my own peace of mind, especially in view of the increased visibility which we encountered as we cruised westward along the Equator. The air was clear as crystal, the sky was cloudless, and the sea was glassy. On our aerial patrols we could easily spot the other task groups when they were twenty or thirty miles away. There was no doubt in any of our minds that the enemy knew of our presence in these waters and was only waiting to see where we would strike before retaliating in strength. We had confirmation of our suspicions the night before the strike when enemy torpedo planes attacked, several being shot down without damage to our ships.

Again we were assigned the combat air patrols over our task group, and again my pilots felt cheated by missing out on the pre-dawn fighter sweeps. "Those darned game-hogs on the big carriers get all the gravy," they complained.

This situation came to a climax after the first flights returned, when three pilots of Lt. Jim Stewart's team came up to me and complained that their other teammate had gone A.W.O.L. from a patrol to horn in on the fighter sweep. "Skipper, we don't want to fly with Jack Wirth any more!" they told me. "He ran off and left us!"

This was a new form of desertion, to leave a comparatively safe post and join a much more dangerous mission, but nevertheless it called for prompt action if air discipline were to be maintained. Calling Wirth to my room, I asked him what it was all about.

"I didn't run off from them, Skipper," he protested. "I just never did find them when we were catapulted for the dawn patrol. It was too dark and there were too many clouds. I saw some planes in the distance and when I joined up they were headed for the target."

"Why didn't you return then, Jack?"

"I was going to, but just then a Zeke made a run on us," he said, using the code word for a Japanese Zero, "and I was afraid to come back alone for fear of getting jumped."

"That sounds reasonable," I said. "Now before you talk to anyone else about this, just sit down here at my desk and write me a play-by-play description of what happened over the target."

Leaving him alone, I returned to the others. "Don't judge him yet," I told them. "He's seen something which scared him plenty, for he's jumpy as a cat."

Before long Wirth reappeared and handed me the following statement:

DETAILS OF ACTION OVER TARGET
AT DAWN 30 MARCH 1944.

I joined up on the first three planes I saw, but these joined two other divisions which went in over the target, where the first sight of enemy planes was a formation of 5 or 6 Zekes at 12 o'clock up, distance about 3 miles. We were at about 7500 feet and the enemy was at 9000 feet. Enemy course was perpendicular to ours. I immediately changed course to converge on them, climbing all the way with full military power. I made a low side run from 4 o'clock on the nearest Zeke which immediately turned toward me and started a tight spiral down to the right. It finally straightened out in a dive and continued pushing over. It was very difficult to get a shot at him because he passed the vertical. He was in this atti-

tude when he hit the ground and I barely pulled out myself.

The second plane I engaged was another Zeke which I saw emerge from a cloud at about 10 o'clock down. My altitude was about 8000 feet, his about 7000 feet. I turned toward him, nosing down, and was closing rapidly when he must have seen me. He turned away, evidently to get back in cloud cover. I closed to about 300 yards and opened fire with 6 guns until I was fairly close. At about 100 yards, he seemed to fall apart all of a sudden and I pulled up in order not to hit the flying debris. I recollect a wing section coming toward me.

Between this action and ensuing action with enemy aircraft, I responded to a call for cover for TBF's and SB2C's. They said Zekes were after them so I descended rapidly in the direction of the lagoon. It was about 5 miles from where I engaged the last enemy plane. I accompanied some TBF's on an attack and strafed an AK (cargo ship) with 4 guns, then acted as cover for some TBF's retiring toward the rendezvous point. As they entered a rain squall, I saw a Zeke obviously preparing to intercept the TBF's on the other side of the squall. I pulled up in the clear and headed for the Zeke but lost him. When I had *gained about 7000 feet altitude, I saw a Hamp level and to my left about 9 o'clock. He also turned away but I closed on him slowly. As I was about to open fire, he turned to the left and I in turn swung inside and opened fire with 6 guns. I saw my bullets hit in the cockpit area on the second burst; my first was not on but behind due to insufficient lead. When my bullets were hitting, they would sparkle brilliantly and he pushed over in a dive. I got about two more bursts into him on this dive and he was past the vertical when he entered a cloud at 2000 feet. I had turned during the dive and recovered in a cloud going in the opposite direction from the enemy. I do not claim a kill on this Hamp but I do claim a probable because in my estimation it would have been impossible for him to recover.*

Our speed was about 350 knots indicated when he entered the cloud and I broke off pursuit. After this action, I joined with another fighter and returned to base.

Between my first and second action I was attacked by a Hamp. I executed a tight 360° nose-down turn when a cannon shell was fired at me. It seemed to pass between the cockpit and the wing and made a noise like a prolonged thump. I believe it passed through my prop arc and in one case it

*looked like a fiery baseball. As I straight-
ened out from my first turn I was again fired
on from behind and I tried a tight turn to
the left. As I recall, I straightened out and
was fired on again, by one cannon shell. I
became frantic and thinking escape impossible, I pulled the stick straight back with
two hands and kicked hard right rudder.
I was indicating about 200 knots and the
plane went into a snap roll and out of control, as I must have held the stick back for
about three turns. I finally recovered after
going through thin clouds and leveled off.
The Hamp was gone, and I came on back
alone.*

*I further certify that this account is true
and accurate to the best of my knowledge.
I'm still confused on some aspects but in
general this is what occurred.*

J. L. WIRTH
LT. (jg) U.S.N.

From this account it was evident that Wirth had shot
down two Zekes and had probably destroyed one
Hamp. He was visibly shaken as the result of his narrow escape from the Hamp on his tail, and his neck
was stiff and sore from the violent evasive action he
had taken, luckily without snapping his wings off. I
believed his story, but his team-mates were still so resentful that they demanded proof of his kills either from

witnesses or by camera gun films. Of course no witnesses were available, and a bad job of developing a poor batch of films exposed in weak light cheated Wirth of photographic confirmation. The ship's Air Officer settled the matter with an edict that no credit would be allowed for planes shot down by pilots who left their assigned stations. Wirth's only comment was, "Damn 'em, I'll show 'em yet!"

After the enemy's fighters had been cleaned out, the Palau strike followed the pattern of our previous raids, with bombing and strafing attacks on the shipping in the lagoon and the shore installations on Peleliu, Angaur, Koror, and Babelthaup islands. Two of our fighter pilots made a strafing run on a light cruiser, which to their amazement headed for shore and ran itself aground, apparently beached by its captain to avoid being sunk in deep water. Most of the shipping spotted by earlier reconnaissance flights had been pulled out before our arrival. We suspected that the same strategy was being used by the enemy to save his airplanes, in view of the proximity of the big Philippine air base at Davao to the west and Yap to the northeast.

This proved to be the case, as we were to learn before many hours had passed.

Grand Slam

MY ROOM-MATE on the ship, until I had inherited the air group commander's single privacy, was the Fighter Director Officer, Lt. Comdr. Pat Rooney. Pat had picked up a touch of malaria on Guadalcanal that put him in a deck job, which irked him no end. He was a good F.D.O., and he ran his interceptions with an Irish enthusiasm that made even the practice runs as much fun as hunting quail with a good bird-dog.

Pat's lair in the Combat Information Center was Radar Plot, a fantastic nest of unbelievable electrical gadgets, radio telephones, noise, and weird charts. From all this apparent confusion Pat sifted out the vital information we needed to protect our ships from aerial attack, relaying it to the combat air patrols overhead and dispatching the fighters to intercept any suspect aircraft detected by the ship's radar, which may be described loosely as an electrical divining rod capable of locating a metal object, such as a ship or an airplane, at a considerable distance.

At the close of the first day's strikes on Palau I was leading an eight-plane combat air patrol over our task group, which was retiring to the east about a hundred miles southeast of the target. We had made the usual routine interceptions of returning patrols for an hour or so when Pat's voice came through my earphones with a ring to it that told me beyond doubt that something unusual was up.

"Hello, Topaz One-One, this is Topaz Base: vector two-four-zero, liner!"

Heading in the direction indicated, I acknowledged his instructions: "Hello, Topaz Base: Topaz One-One on vector."

He then gave me code instructions which gave me the approximate distance and direction of the bogey. Since we had no forces in the area indicated, we could only assume that it was either one of our own long-range search planes or that enemy planes were headed our way.

"What size bogey?" I asked him, for he had sent only my division, retaining the other four planes over the task group.

"Bogey small," he answered. "Either one big plane or two or three small planes."

This looked interesting, unless it turned out to be another Liberator going in for damage assessment photographs with flash bombs. I checked my gun switches and turned on my electrical gun sight. Pat gave us several changes of direction to merge our course with that of the enemy. Nooy was flying on my left, with Wilson and Hancock to the right, all of us scanning the sky in the direction indicated.

Again Pat's voice reached us, resonant with suppressed excitement: "Vector port, thirty degrees, buster! Look down—bogey may be below you!"

Before I could answer there was a shout from Nooy: "Tallyho! Bandits at ten o'clock down!"

"Go get 'em!" I called, giving him the lead.

Nooy banked sharply to port, heading in the direction he had indicated. As soon as he straightened out I spotted our quarry, and the sight of them almost took the breath out of me. Instead of the two or three planes I had expected, there was a neat formation of small, sleek planes in a V of V's—at least three times our number, apparently fighters.

"Amplify tallyho report!" Rooney reminded us.

"Many planes, all bogies!" answered Nooy, forgetting in his excitement to state what type.

By this time I was close enough to the enemy formation to make an estimate of their number and indicate their type—vital information to the task group in case they got through.

"Nine rats!" I answered. "All Zekes!"

We were at seventeen thousand feet, diving on the enemy formation about two thousand feet below us. I felt a momentary resentment at the limitations of radar which had permitted no warning that we were outnumbered, but felt that the only way to whittle down the odds was to get as many of the enemy as possible before they knew we were around. Accordingly I cut in below Nooy and headed for the leader of the Japanese formation.

For a moment we had the advantage of surprise while we attacked with the sun behind us, but before I was near enough to fire I saw the leading V of three planes pull off to the left from the rest of the formation, evidently to counter my attack.

Here we go! I thought. *They were just waiting for us to rush in. I wonder how many more of them are waiting upstairs?*

Taking as much of a lead as I could get on the plane nearest to me, I fired a short preliminary burst at extreme range for a sighting shot. To my amazement the plane instantly burst into flames and started down. This left the leader and his starboard wingman.

Zooming upward to save my excess speed, I glanced up and around to see how I stood, with a mingled feeling of relief and surprise to find no Zekes on my tail. Off to the right my three team-mates were just starting high side runs on the remainder of the enemy formation, with no escorting planes in sight so far.

Below me the enemy leader and his wingman had nosed over in a high-speed glide, making no attempt to turn and fight—unorthodox conduct for Zekes, but this was no time to wonder about it. Boring down on them at full throttle I made a stern approach on the leader's wingman, again opening fire as soon as I was within a thousand feet. Again there was a spurt of flame at the first burst from my guns, and the plane in my sights was a fiery torch. By shifting my point of aim a few degrees to the left I had the leader under fire on the same run, with the same results. His wing tanks flamed as soon as I fired, and down he plunged to join the others.

All this happened so fast that less than thirty seconds had passed since I had first opened fire until there were no more targets in front of me. I could not believe such luck, nor understand why these Zekes did not turn and try to tear us apart instead of simply trying to run away without even any evasive action.

The answer came to me in a radio call from Wilson, his voice muffled by his oxygen mask: "Skipper! Watch out! These aren't Zekes! They're *Judieth!*"

"They're what?" I asked. "Say again!"

"*Judieth!* You know—that new dive bomber!"

I still could not make out what he said. "Say again!" I told him. "What do you mean?"

He gave up trying to make me understand the name, and warned: "Look out for them; they've got *rear-seat gunners!*"

This brought me up with a jolt. Now I knew what he was trying to tell me. What I had mistaken for single-seat fighters were the Japs' newest and fastest reconnaissance dive bombers which we had given the code name of Judy. They were approximately the same size as the Zeke, with a design so similar that in approaching them from astern I had not seen their in-line liquid-cooled engines. Worse yet, I had not seen their rear-seat gunners, who had undoubtedly seen me, to judge from the bullet holes through my wings which I now noticed for the first time.

"Watch out for fighter cover!" I warned the others,

craning my neck to look above and behind me. Still
there were no fighters around. Glancing down, I saw
half a dozen big oil slicks on the water below us where
most of the enemy formation had splashed.

Nooy and Hancock were chasing two others off to the
west, while Wilson was tailing a single Judy headed
north toward our ships.

"Go get him, Bob!" I told him. "I'll cover your tail."

"Wilco!" he answered, and off we roared at full power
in pursuit.

After a few minutes I had caught up with Wilson,
who was still unable to gain on the fleeing Jap. Apparently my engine had a slight advantage over the
others. Gradually I pulled ahead of Wilson, slowly closing the gap between my plane and the Judy, which
was still headed north just out of range of my guns. By
now we were down to twelve thousand feet, pulling
every inch of manifold pressure we could get out of our
belabored engines without burning them up. Ahead of
us a few degrees to port was a large bank of cumulous
clouds. I thought the Jap was running for this cover,
but he made no attempt to change course. This could
mean only one thing: he had already given up any
thought of getting home, and was looking for a target.
Before long he would have one, for we had chased him
nearly seventy miles and were getting close to our task
force.

With this realization I quit trying to keep from burning out my engine and opened everything wide to get
its last ounce of horsepower. By now the sun was setting

and time was growing short. Still I could not get within range. As a last resort I raised my plane's nose and lobbed a few long-range bursts at the Jap. One of these evidently nicked his engine, for I was then able to close on him. He now took violent evasive action, skidding and slipping from side to side as I closed for the kill, until suddenly he chopped his throttle to make me overshoot so that he could get in a shot with his forward-firing fixed guns. I very nearly rammed him, but managed to pull up just in time to avoid a collision.

At that speed I zoomed half a mile above him before I could level off and roll over to look down. From there I had a grandstand view of what followed. The Jap had entered a steep dive to the right. At first I thought he was finished, but soon it was obvious that he had a definite objective in view. Then I saw it—one of our picket destroyers steaming along all alone several miles from the task force.

It was a suicide dive, but the Jap was too late. His momentary pause had given Wilson a chance to get within gun range, and halfway to his target the Jap burst into flames and dropped like a meteor into the sea.

Wilson started to circle the spot, but I called him off; I wanted to get out of there before that destroyer's gun crews started to wonder where that flaming airplane had come from and started tossing five-inch ack-ack at us. Heading back toward our task group I called the others to report.

"Three down," replied Wilson.

"I splashed two," said Nooy.

"My guns jammed," said Hancock. "I only got one."

With my three, this made a total of nine. This I reported to the ship: "Hello Topaz Base: nine planes splashed, all Judys."

"Nice going!" answered Rooney. "A grand slam!"

Nooy and Hancock, flying back together to join us, evidently had seen other planes.

"There were more than nine," said Nooy. "Some were Tonys."

This put us on the alert again. As Wilson and I circled the task force at five thousand feet I spotted two planes low on the water, flying very fast and headed parallel to the course of our ships. Signalling for Wilson to follow me I started a high-speed dive to investigate. The two planes turned and headed south. Off to my left I saw two other Hellcats from another task group joining the chase.

This time the Japs had the better engines. Try as we would, we could not close the interval. The two Judys got right down on the surface of the ocean and never changed course. After about ten minutes we saw big splashes under them; evidently they had jettisoned their bomb loads. Thus lightened they began to pull away from us. Again I tried to force them to turn by lobbing a few bursts at them, but each time I pulled up my plane's nose to fire I lost a little more distance. The sun had now set, and after we had chased them about forty miles I gave it up as a hopeless job.

"Knock it off," I called to Wilson, who still wanted to follow them. Our fuel was getting so low after nearly an hour at full throttle that we would have to return to the ship at once. The two Judys had jettisoned their bombs, and they were too far from land to have any chance to get back after burning up most of their fuel supply to escape.

We got back aboard on our reserve fuel tanks, and Rooney met us in the ready room.

"I still say it's a grand slam," he said with a grin. "Those buzzards will never get home from where you chased 'em. Nine shot down and two others lost at sea— not a bad hour's work!"

The other pilots were as resentful as if we had intentionally cheated them of their natural rights. "Your division always gets the gravy hops!" they protested. "How about giving someone else a chance to shoot something once in a while?"

Instead of answering, my wingmen just grinned happily.

Captain Schoeffel sent me a note which was better than a medal:

> OUR C.A.P. RECEIVED A "WELL DONE" FROM
> THE TASK FORCE FIGHTER DIRECTOR. CON-
> GRATULATIONS. PLEASE INFORM YOUR PILOTS.
> ROONEY TELLS ME YOUR RADIO DISCIPLINE
> WAS PERFECT. I AM VERY PLEASED.   —M.F.S.

April Fool's Day

DURING THE NIGHT the Japs ferried in more fighters from their airfields in the Philippines, and our dawn patrol was scrambled singly to intercept bogies on the way in. Again the pre-dawn fighter sweeps from the other carriers saw all the action, this time with more enemy air opposition than had been encountered on the previous day. Once more it was a one-sided affair, with the sky soon cleared of enemy fighters so that the Avengers and Helldivers could get in their Sunday punches with bombs and torpedoes. This they did so thoroughly that by the middle of the afternoon the remaining strikes were called off for lack of worth-while targets, and the task force started its retirement. That night the *Cabot* received a message from the task group commander which Captain Schoeffel passed on to me:

WELL DONE ON YOUR WORK ON THE ATTACKS
LAST NIGHT.

Altogether the Palau strike had been a very successful operation.

The following day we hit the enemy's base on the

island of Wolei while another task group hit their staging base on the island of Yap northeast of Palau. This was a routine operation, with no aerial opposition over Wolei and not even any anti-aircraft fire to hinder our pilots as they demolished the island's ground installations and pitted its airfield with bomb craters. Only one enemy airplane was seen during the entire day, and it was shot down by one of my boys after a comedy of errors which did justice to the date of the action—April First.

On that morning the first two combat air patrols had encountered no snoopers. I had taken the ten o'clock patrol for my division, to avoid any criticism of hogging the earlier patrols which were usually the most productive. We had two divisions circling over the task group at ten thousand feet, with several Avengers out on the low-altitude anti-submarine patrols. The other fighter division was the controversial team composed of Stewart, Hawkins, Wirth, and Hayde.

We had been on station less than half an hour when Pat Rooney reported a low-flying bogey to the east of the task group. Much to the resentment of my wingmen, as evidenced by their pantomimed expressions of chagrin, Rooney dispatched Stewart's team to make the interception. The bogey was reported in the search sector being covered by "Beast" Russell of our torpedo squadron, who immediately took over the job of keeping the ship informed of whatever progress was being made when the radio reports became garbled.

The air was so clear that the bogey was sighted about

ten miles away by Jack Wirth, who gave a tallyho that
would have made a Chippewa chief green with envy.
The bogey was soon identified as a Japanese Betty medium bomber, probably sent out from Truk to snoop on
our activities. From that moment the radio reports really
became garbled, and The Beast went into his act.

All we could hear from the pursuers was a mad jumble
of shouts, profanity, and what sounded like war whoops.
Back on the ship Pat Rooney demanded a progress report, which The Beast promptly supplied from his own
interpretation of what was being said.

"They say they're chasing Bettys!" he announced.

Even this transmission was interfered with by the
commotion on the other end of the circuit. Rooney got
only the first part of it.

"Say again!" he requested.

"They're chasing Bettys!" repeated The Beast.

"I understand you say sixteen Bettys," said Rooney.
"Is that correct?"

During this transmission the confusion doubled, but
The Beast heard part of it.

"That is correct," he answered. "They are chasing
Bettys!"

That was enough for Rooney. He turned in the alarm
and the ship went to General Quarters. The pilots left
aboard roared their protests as they rushed to the ready
room: "Sixteen Bettys, and the Skipper's division's in
the air! He did it on purpose!"

By this time even my wingmen were convinced that
they were missing out on something, and they bounced

around my plane indicating plainly that they wanted to go to the fire. I held them back, having heard the original conversation, until we got a report from Stewart: "Splashed one Betty, returning to base."

This ended the commotion, and the *Cabot* secured from General Quarters. Back aboard at the end of the flight we learned that the mad race to massacre the lone Betty had been won by Frank Hayde, who had laboriously waxed and polished his Hellcat's wings for days in anticipation of this very situation, thereby gaining a knot or two on his team-mates. For the rest of that cruise, Hayde was known as "the Ace of Wolei."

From Wolei back to Majuro the cruise was uneventful. There was not even any bad weather to break the monotony. The tropical and equatorial fronts, sources of most of the rainy weather around the Equator, had retired to the south, leaving the ocean lake-smooth.

AFTER A COUPLE OF WEEKS in Majuro lagoon we were again on the warpath, this time with New Guinea as our destination. Our force sortied on the thirteenth of April and spent nearly a week cruising down to the area from which our strikes were to be launched. Our particular targets were three airfields several miles inland beyond a high ridge of mountains between Humboldt Bay and Tanamerah Bay. These airfields, named Hollandia, Sentani, and Cyclops, were the chief staging bases for Japanese air power along the northern New Guinea coast. They lay along the shores of Lake Sentani, a large body of crocodile-infested water in the midst of some of the worst terrain in the southwest Pacific Ocean areas—malaria-ridden, covered with tall saw-grass and rain-forest, and inhabited by savages who were not only unfriendly to both sides, but were reputed to be cannibals as well as head-hunters. For once every pilot listened attentively to every word of the briefings on jungle survival, for it would be hard to imagine a more unpleasant place for a forced landing. In addition to this we ran into bad weather for the first time during a strike—low clouds, driving rain, and poor visibility which prevented the usual pre-dawn fighter sweep from being launched.

In spite of this inauspicious beginning, the first day's operations were unopposed. By mid-morning the weather improved and the first strikes reported no opposition over the target. The area had been so thoroughly covered by previous Army bombing strikes that very few undamaged Japanese planes could be located even on the ground.

On one strike I was leading the fighter cover for the dive bombers and torpedo planes, strafing the airfields after the bombs had been dropped, when someone reported three enemy bombers sighted over Humboldt Bay. Immediately every fighter pilot in the vicinity headed for the area indicated, hoping to get there before someone else made the kill. The Jap planes turned out to be twin-engined Nells, low on the water, heading west along the rocky coast trying to reach safety.

One of the first pilots to reach the scene was Jack Wirth, who dived in at full speed and drew a bead on the nearest Nell. Just as he was about to press his trigger a stream of tracers poured past his wing into the Jap plane, which burst into flames. Someone had cut in ahead of Wirth to beat him to the draw. Shifting to another Nell, Wirth again prepared to fire, only to see this plane also flamed by someone else's guns. Three times he tried, but each time another Hellcat cut him out of a kill. Wirth came back aboard muttering to himself, very disgusted with the injustice of it all. No other enemy planes were airborne near the target.

The next day our attention was shifted to other airfields a hundred miles or so along the coast west of Hollandia. Two of these were Wakde and Sawar, staging fields for the bigger airfields around Hollandia. Here my boys got a bit too cocky, strafing the enemy planes and gun emplacements they found hidden under the coconut palms on Wakde Island. Wirth's engine was hit by small-caliber gunfire from the ground, and he barely made it back to the vicinity of the ship when he was forced to make a water landing. He was picked up by a destroyer which returned him after demanding twenty gallons of ice cream for his ransom.

On one flight, Scales and Bowie were cruising along the coastline when they spotted a ship hidden in a cove, a thousand-ton oiler which the Japanese had cleverly camouflaged to protect their dwindling fuel supply. A few strafing runs set it afire, and in a short time a black pall of smoke hung over Hollandia.

On another flight near Samar, two pilots reported hearing the following radio conversation by two planes over some other airfield:

"Look! There's a Zeke about to take off!"

"Let's go down and get him!"

"Hell no! Let him take off first. They don't count unless they're airborne!"

That was the way they fought, tearing into anything that moved, rushing in regardless of the odds. In many cases they were protected only by the safety that goes with aggressive offense, when the enemy must have thought that the attacking planes were only the vanguard of a much superior force. More than once this aggressiveness paid big dividends, and brought our pilots through tight situations where the score could easily have been reversed.

After our amphibious troops were all ashore around Hollandia the task force turned away and steamed north. All conjecture as to our next destination was soon ended when it was casually announced that on our way back to Majuro we were going to take a passing slap at Truk, just to show the Japs that the first walloping we had given their prize stronghold was not merely a matter of luck.

As one pilot expressed it: "If we don't stay away from Truk, the first thing we know the Japs will be charging us docking fees!"

Truk Again

THIS TIME we approached Truk from the west, and this time the Japs knew we were coming. Half a dozen snoopers were shot down by the combat air patrols on the way north, so that we knew the enemy had been well alerted. In spite of this the pre-dawn fighter sweeps were launched without interference, and when the sun came up we were only about seventy miles southwest of Truk itself.

"This is too close!" complained one pilot. "We're only inviting them to come out and nail us!"

As if in answer to his prediction the general alarm gong started clanging away. The loudspeaker soon gave the reason: "Large bogey closing from the east. Scramble all available fighters!"

Rushing up to the flight deck, I found Hawkins already seated in the Hellcat on the catapult. He pretended not to see me. The next two Hellcats were also occupied. When I started to climb into the next, Frank Hayde's head popped up from inside the cockpit where he was checking his oxygen. I motioned for him to get out. His face contorted as he replied something that was unintelligible in the roar of the engines being started around us, but it was obviously something unprintable. I gave him a reassuring pat on the back and looked for another plane. Every plane was occupied, and every occupant cursed me if I so much as touched the airplane.

Only three planes had been catapulted when the order was given to cut all engines. Over the bull-horn came a warning: "Enemy torpedo planes broad on the starboard beam! All pilots clear the flight deck!"

Joining the other disappointed pilots I headed for the ready room. Before we were halfway along the flight deck the ship's 40-mm. guns started firing. Half a dozen enemy torpedo planes, Kates or Jills, had broken through our destroyer screen and were now boring in low on the water, right in the middle of our force. Two made a run on one of the large carriers next to us and were shot down by its anti-aircraft batteries. Cruiser and battleship guns accounted for all the rest except one which flew right on through the hail of tracers around it. Above this plane swooped one of the Hellcats we had just catapulted, ignoring the flak being tossed up around it, following every turn the Jap made. This was Hawkins, who caught the enemy plane before it could drop its torpedo and splashed it inside of the destroyer screen. Hayde chased another Kate and splashed it a few miles north of the task force. The attack was smashed without damage to our ships, unbelievably.

Meanwhile the fighter sweep was getting in its best licks, and before long all aerial opposition over the target was eliminated, with over a hundred planes destroyed in the air and on the ground. Now the task force settled down to the primary mission of the attack, which was the destruction of Japanese shore installations. All day long we lugged heavy bombs in and dumped them on Truk's airfields, hangars, repair shops, and administration buildings. Even the fighters assigned to cover the big Avengers and Helldivers carried 1000-pound bombs.

This time the anti-aircraft fire was more accurate, for the Japs had profited by our previous raid to correct their aim. One of our Hellcats was hit in the engine but managed to limp back most of the way before ditching. The pilot, Ensign Galt, was rescued by a destroyer.

One pilot who looked behind him as he pulled out of a strafing dive said he'd never look back again, and that if he had known how many guns were shooting at him he would never have gone near the blamed island in the first place.

Our A.C.I. officer asked one pilot whether the anti-aircraft fire was heavy or light.

"I'd call it light;" he answered, "none came near me."

His wingman had other ideas. "I got three holes in my plane," he said. "That stuff really jolted me. *I'd* call it *heavy!*"

Like anything else, it all depended on the point of view.

On one dive we had to pull out past a high hill on Dublon Island which was packed with medium-caliber ack-ack installations. I had just left my bomb in a cluster of buildings along the northwest tip of the island, pull-

ing out along the shoreline to the east. Never before
had I seemed to see the ground go by beneath me so
slowly, although I was making around four hundred
miles an hour at the time. I noticed details of buildings
and terrain on the hillside as it slid by under me, such
as the excessively large number of buildings marked
with the red cross, thinking that if we could believe the
Japs, half of their buildings on Dublon Island were hos-
pitals.

By the second day of the strike everyone really got
into the spirit of the thing. Truk was taking a beating
which should have a profound effect upon its Japanese
proprietors. Every bomb that was loaded onto our
planes bore some message chalked on it by the various
plane captains, armament crews, plane handlers, or gun
crews. Most of these were of the same general tone—a
derisive message with signatures of the senders and their
friends, sweethearts, or relatives. Here are a few I
copied down at random:

"For Tojo, from Pop, Mom, Bud, Gloria, and Jackie."

"If this don't go off we will send you another one.
Marge, Joyce, Wilma Lee and Lou, Mary and Cath-
erine."

"Excuse my bust. From the Gas House Boys, for Rita,
Olga, Alice, Tessie."

"For mother on her birthday. Olga, Dinah, Estelle,
Wilma send compliments. More later!"

All of these messages were cheerfully delivered, but
it is very doubtful if any of them were legible upon arrival.

On the afternoon of the second day a thick overcast closed in over the target, and the later strikes were cancelled. Once more we turned toward the east and headed back to our anchorage at Majuro. Again a pencilled note from Captain Schoeffel was handed to me by his orderly:

> PLEASE EXPRESS TO THE PERSONNEL OF BOTH SQUADRONS FOR ME MY APPRECIATION OF A FINE JOB. IT WAS IN NO SENSE YOUR FAULT THAT THERE WAS SO LITTLE OPPOSITION. HAD THERE BEEN MORE I AM SURE YOU WOULD HAVE SMASHED IT.
>
> THE ADMIRAL HAS JUST SENT THE TASK GROUP A "WELL DONE." SO FAR AS I KNOW THIS IS THE SECOND TIME HE HAS EVER SENT SUCH A MESSAGE, THE OTHER TIME BEING YOUR GRAND SLAM.   —M.F.S.

On the way back to Majuro our battlewagons and cruisers pulled out of the formation long enough to give the Japs on Ponape and Kusaie a thorough shellacking with their big guns. At Majuro we received our first mail from home in several weeks. Among other letters I found one from my local draft board which stated that it had no record of my having registered with it or with any other draft board, and directing me to register at once with the nearest board. My yeoman wanted to write them that they could not get me in the Army, no matter how hard they tried, but when I pointed out that this would snarl up their records and waste someone's time tracing me as a draft dodger, he reluctantly prepared a more conventional acknowledgment.

This time our stay in Majuro posed a real morale problem, for we were to wait there for over a month while our amphibious forces completed the occupation of the Hollandia area and regrouped for the next series of landings. War is mostly waiting, but this was the longest period of inactivity we had yet had to sit out. Unable to fly because of the congestion ashore, we had to provide other forms of activity for our pilots to keep them from going completely stale. They began to refer to the monotonous routine of lying at anchor in a tropical lagoon as "the Bore War."

Luckily I had anticipated such a reaction and had ordered a stock of sports equipment suitable for tropical recreation, including fishing gear, underwater face masks, fish spears, swimming fins, shotguns with portable clay pigeon throwers, and beer for picnics ashore. We had all kinds of athletic equipment aboard for such sports as volleyball, badminton, deck tennis, and basketball, and I had two sets of sixteen-ounce boxing gloves with which we used to pound each other around the flight deck.

Every pilot was required to take part in some form of competitive exercise each day. Nets were rigged from booms over the side for swimming in the lagoon, and inter-ship leagues were formed in basketball and volleyball to keep up the interest and the spirit of competition. My boys claimed the Fleet championship in basketball and volleyball after trimming previously unbeaten teams aboard the *Enterprise* which were the pride and joy of Commander Tom Hamilton, famed Naval Academy athlete and football coach. Such activities not only kept our pilots in shape but also encouraged the aggressive spirit so necessary in a fighting squadron.

Toward the end of May we received word that we would be off again on the fifth of June, and this time no one was very much surprised to learn that our objective was the occupation of the Marianas Islands, to provide airfields from which new long-range land-based bombers could attack Japan itself. These bombers, already in production, were the famous B-29's, or Superfortresses. The operations plan frankly stated that a surface action with the Japanese fleet was expected, as the enemy could not afford to let us get a foothold so close to his home islands and would undoubtedly do everything in his power to prevent such an invasion. The success or failure of this operation would be the turning point of the war in the Pacific. Upon learning this, the consensus among our pilots was expressed in three words: "This is *it!*"

After our long stretch of aerial inactivity every pilot was restless and spoiling for a good fight. There is something about flying which is more than a habit and at times almost a vice; grounded pilots grow irritable and grouchy. Quarrels and even fistfights are frequently the climax of long periods of enforced idleness. In addition to this, we were all looking forward to action over the Marianas airfields which we had missed on the previous

carrier strikes in February when we had escorted the
Intrepid back to Pearl Harbor.

A few days before we were scheduled to depart, the
ship's communications officer received a dispatch which
he brought to my room and handed to me without comment. The message directed that I be detached in June
or July to report to the Navy Department in Washington by first available air transportation. This could only
mean another desk job. I begged the communications
officer to hide it and say nothing about it until after we
were at sea. This he consented to do, since Captain
Schoeffel was being relieved and Commander Washburn was also expected to be detached. This meant a
promotion for both officers, the former to the flag rank
of rear admiral and the latter to a captaincy with command of another aircraft carrier, the *Lunga Point*. Pat
Patterson had already been detached to form a fighter
squadron for an escort carrier. In the midst of the general confusion I got away with it, and was still aboard
when we weighed anchor and steamed out of Majuro's
lagoon for the last time. From now on we were to use
other anchorages closer to Tokyo. Our offensive was
really getting into high gear at last.

Daylight Fighter Sweep

LUCK WAS WITH US most of the way out to the
northwest of Truk. The first Japanese snooper plane
was a twin-engined Betty, shot down by one of our four-
engined Liberators which were patrolling ahead of us.
This was a real break, for it enabled the task force to
get in much closer than if the interception had been
made by carrier fighters. No matter how quickly the
fighters make their kill, the snooper's radio operator
usually has time to get off one last frantic signal telling
his home base that carrier-based planes are attacking
in his search sector. That always gives away the show,
for carrier-based planes in the vicinity inevitably mean
that fleet units are on the prowl.

But then the inevitable happened. Another Betty
snooper came into range and fighters from one of our
combat air patrols were sent out to get it. This Betty
played hide-and-seek in the clouds for some time before
the Hellcats knocked it down, so that there was no doubt
that a contact report had tipped the Japs off to the fact
that we were well on our way to the Marianas. The fat
was in the fire.

Everyone realized that this strike would be different from any previous assignments in that we would be operating within range of more enemy airfields than ever before. Since the first hit-and-run strike on Saipan, Tinian, and Guam four months before, reconnaissance photographs had showed that the Japs were feverishly building new airfields throughout the Marianas, whose terrain is much more suitable for airfield construction than either the Caroline or the Marshall Islands. These new fields were surrounded with airplanes of all types, including several new and improved models in the dive-bomber and torpedo-bomber categories. If the enemy should decide to commit his carrier-based air strength in conjunction with his land-based airplanes to oppose us, he might be able to "saturate" our defenses. Unless somebody figured out a way to break up this possible combination, we might find ourselves in a tight corner.

We had only two days of cruising to go before reaching our objective when a destroyer came alongside the *Cabot* to deliver a special mail packet from the task force commander, Vice Admiral Marc A. Mitscher. In it we found an alternate plan of attack which if carried out successfully might catch the Japs flat-footed. This plan, although unorthodox when compared with our previous operations and obviously a daring and hazardous undertaking, immediately caught the imagination of every pilot aboard. Previous carrier strikes had followed the usual pattern of a dawn fighter sweep to clean out enemy air opposition over the target before the slower and heavier torpedo planes and dive bombers arrived. The first carrier strike on the Marianas had been intercepted the night before the attack, and had to fight off enemy torpedo-plane raids during its pre-dawn launchings when the task force was most vulnerable.

The new plan called for an *afternoon* fighter sweep, to be launched on the day before we planned to attack, in an attempt to decimate the enemy's land-based air strength before his aircraft carriers could get close enough for a coordinated attack. Some of the Jap carriers were known to be near the Philippines, and others would undoubtedly steam down at full speed from their bases in the Empire. From our present distance the Japs would be braced for an attack the following day, and if we hit them twelve hours earlier it might throw them badly off balance, so that the resulting confusion would make our first landings on Saipan much less costly. By steaming in at full speed we could get close enough to launch fighters by midafternoon the next day for a long-range strike, and to recover them again by sunset. It was a daring plan.

Each carrier was to furnish a certain percentage of its fighters for this sweep, retaining an ample number aboard to carry out the original invasion plan even if this attack miscarried. The *Cabot* was to furnish three four-plane combat teams of Hellcats. Every pilot in the fighter squadron was eager to go, for fighter sweeps had become the most sought-after assignments in carrier aviation. By now it was apparent that the pilots who got in on these flights usually saw all of the combat action, while those on subsequent flights seldom saw an enemy plane airborne. After five months in the combat zone, more than half of my fighter pilots had never had a shot at an enemy plane. The reason for this was that the big carriers, having more planes available and thus better able to withstand losses, were usually assigned the fighter sweeps, while the CVL's usually provided fighter cover for the dive bombers and torpedo planes or combat air patrols over the task force. Thus very few of the planes from CVL's were made available for the fighter sweeps, to the disgust of their pilots.

Ordinarily I had tried to arrange for such assignments to be rotated, so that each team would get its chance at combat action, but on this particular strike I decided to take only the three teams with combat experience against enemy fighters, including my own four-man team. When I announced this decision there were some very disappointed expressions on the faces of those pilots who had expected to go, but I explained that this was to be the longest flight ever attempted for such a mission by carrier-based fighters, and that while no reflection on the flying ability of the other teams was intended, the importance of this mission required the assignment of the teams with the most combat experience.

That afternoon a dispatch from the flagship ordered all air group commanders to report aboard for a conference on the coming strike, and I was catapulted for the short flight to the flag carrier. In this conference I found that our squadron was to be given the ideal assignment of top cover on the way in to the target, with instructions to drop out and take care of any enemy aircraft which might be encountered en route. At the target we were to fly medium cover, with two layers of fighters from other carriers above us to keep enemy fighters off our tails while we covered the first wave of strafing planes below us. Our target was the big bomber base on Ushi Point at the north tip of Tinian. Other squadrons were to hit Saipan, Rota and Guam at the same time. Most of the usual additional hazards were absent: the approaches were unobstructed, and there was no reef-surrounded lagoon to fall into, as at Truk and Palau, or cannibal-infested jungle, as at Hollandia. The palm trees which masked the grounded planes at Wakde and Sawar were absent; this was beautiful open farmland with almost no natural cover. If forced down here we could expect friendly forces in the vicinity shortly which might pick us up. Better yet, it was now estimated that we could run in much closer than originally anticipated before launching, so that we would not be tired out by a long flight before fighting. Best of all, the weather forecast was favorable, with a high overcast that would be a perfect background for spotting enemy planes overhead before they could use an altitude advantage. This sounded very encouraging to me as I recalled the fighting in the half-light of that cloudy dawn over Roi, with its nightmarish quality of dim silhouettes which could not be distinguished as friend or foe until we were close enough to see their insignia. Compared with that experience, a midafter-noon engagement was something to look forward to.

Back aboard the *Cabot* I hurried down to the ready room and gave the pilots a quick summary of our revised plan. This was received enthusiastically by the pilots assigned to the flight but with long faces and deep gloom by the others, who felt cheated and insulted.

"All right, cuss me out if you feel like it," I told them, trying to laugh off their disappointment.

"Shall we start now, Skipper, or wait until you're out of the room?" asked one pilot with exaggerated def-erence.

"Now, don't take it so hard," I told them. "There'll be other fighter sweeps."

"Not like this one!" they chorused resentfully.

Lt. Al Mencin, my new executive officer, called me aside. "The boys are really taking it hard," he told me. "They feel that the teams you picked aren't the best in the squadron but only the luckiest, and that they all deserve a break on this one."

"Then we'd better hear what they have to say," I an-swered, turning back to the assembled squadron. "Go ahead and speak up. Get it off your chests."

A twenty-one-year-old ensign stood up. "Captain," he said, "we've been on five major strikes since January, and if you can't trust us on a daylight flight like this, we might as well put in for ferry duty."

"That's right!" agreed the rest in unison.

"This is the safest strike we've had yet," said another pilot.

"Don't be a game-hog, Skipper," pleaded another. "Remember the luck you had at Palau! How about giving someone else a chance to score?"

These were reasonable arguments. If we didn't spread this experience around, we would end up with an unbalanced organization.

Someone volunteered a suggestion: "Let's draw straws for it!"

"Fair enough," I agreed. "The flight surgeon will pick the numbers out of a hat, and the first three teams he picks will make the trip."

"How about eliminating the teams which already have planes to their credit?" suggested another pilot hopefully, but he was immediately howled down by a dozen others, including my three wingmen.

"Nothing doing!" I decided. "We all want a chance at this one. Go ahead, Doc. Draw out three numbers."

The flight surgeon picked three slips from the hat. "The teams to go will be the Third, Fourth, and Fifth," he announced.

This news was received with whoops of delight by the winners and loud groans by the losers. However, it was a good cross-section of the squadron. Only one pilot of the twelve selected, Lt. Doug Mulcahy, twenty-six years old, had shot down a Jap plane. I designated him as leader of the strike. The other two team leaders were both experienced hands, Lt. "Whitey" Turner, twenty-six years old, who had been on escort carrier duty in the Atlantic, and Lt. Steve Kona, twenty-seven, a former member of the famous "Grim Reaper" fighter squadron which saw action with the *Enterprise*. I spent the rest of the day going over every detail of the operations with the pilots who were to make the flight the next day.

Sunday, June 11, 1944, was one of the most ideal days I have ever seen for aerial combat. As we approached the target from the east the sea was almost calm, the visibility unlimited, and a high thin overcast provided a white background which made airplanes at a great distance immediately stand out as black silhouettes. For once recognition was not going to be a problem—for either side!

Our planes took off as scheduled, joined up quickly with the rest of the striking group, and headed west. We could see them almost to the horizon. The next few hours I spent sitting by the radio, straining to hear any word which might indicate how my boys were making out, but they were out of range. The first indication we had that they were on their way back was when they announced that they had sighted us and were preparing to land. All of us rushed up to the flight deck to count them as they made their check-in pass along the port side—four, eight, ten, eleven—where was that twelfth plane? One pilot, Ensign Dick Whitworth, twenty-four, was missing from his usual position in the formation. Another plane had a large ragged hole through its wing. We saw a splash upwind ahead of us, where a fighter had just made a water landing ahead of a destroyer, which changed course to pick up the pilot.

The first pilot back aboard was "Salty" Galt, who

grinned and held up two fingers to indicate two Jap planes shot down. He had taken over the lead shortly after the takeoff, when Mulcahy's radio went bad. Galt had an old score to settle with the Japs, for it was he who had been shot down by anti-aircraft fire over Truk a few weeks earlier, to spend several days on the destroyer which picked him up. The pilot with the hole in his wing was Lt. (jg) Dan Driscoll, twenty-three, who made a good landing with one flat tire which was riddled by gunfire. He also got two Zeros, although one of these ventilated his wing with a 20-mm. cannon shell and punched a steel slug halfway through the armor plate behind his back. Lt. (jg) Dick Conant, twenty-two, was bleeding from cuts along his face and neck made by flying fragments when a Jap bullet pierced his cockpit canopy right behind his ear. Lt. (jg) Ed Free, twenty-one, had strafed and burned a giant four-engined Jap bomber of a new type on the field at Ushi Point.

Steve Kona had taken photographs of this and other burning planes, including two twin-engined bombers which he had strafed. He also shot down a Zeke. Whitey Turner was high man with two sure and two probable victories in the air. Every pilot scored either in the air or on the ground, the final tally showing thirteen Jap fighters shot down, three probably shot down and two damaged in the air, with four destroyed and fourteen damaged on the ground, for a total of thirty-six enemy planes destroyed or damaged. Not a bad hour's work for twelve pilots!

The only dark spot in the day's performance was that

Dick Whitworth was still missing. The pilot who made the water landing ahead of us was from another carrier. Whitworth had last been seen during a wild melee over Tinian. The Japs had got the jump on our pilots, having been waiting with twenty or thirty fighters above them in the thin overcast. In spite of this initial disadvantage, my boys broke up the enemy's attack, pounced on the disorganized strays, and destroyed every enemy plane in the air before strafing those on the ground. Several Japs had bailed out after their planes caught fire, and at one time there were four parachutes in the air, drifting down over the sea to the west of Tinian. Most of these were Japs, but Galt had shot down a Zeke as it started a strafing run on one parachute, so that we did not give up hope for Whitworth, who was in good shape and as tough as they come.

It should be remembered that this was the first plane-to-plane combat action for most of these pilots—the first time they had ever fired a gun at an enemy plane in the air. They not only had volunteered for this mission, but had literally demanded it.

This initial success permitted our task force to launch its pre-invasion strikes the next morning without having to fight off a large-scale enemy air attack and without damage to a single ship. The immobility of Japan's "unsinkable island aircraft carriers" had once more proved to be a liability when pitted against the mobile, flexible attack of a fast-striking carrier task force.

Four days later, as we patrolled the coast of Saipan while the battleships and cruisers pulverized its coast defenses, we received a message from another task group:

ENSIGN R. G. WHITWORTH PICKED UP BY DE-
STROYER ABOUT 2100 LAST NIGHT IN GOOD
CONDITION. ATTACKED ZEKE AT 8000 FEET
AND WAS ATTACKED BY SECOND ZEKE WHO SET
HIS RIGHT WING TANK AFIRE WITH CANNON
SHELL. MADE WATER LANDING WHEELS UP
FIVE MILES SOUTHWEST OF TINIAN. ZEKE FOL-
LOWED DOWN BUT APPARENTLY UNABLE TO
SEE HIM IN WATER. LIFE RAFT AND STANDARD
EMERGENCY EQUIPMENT EMPLOYED. SHOT
BIRD. STILL HAD EMERGENCY RATIONS AND
WATER WHEN PICKED UP AFTER THREE DAYS
ADRIFT. READY FOR DUTY NOW.

It was a hot day when the destroyer passed Whitworth over to us in a breeches buoy, and the destroyer's crew held out for forty gallons of ice cream. The price of pilots was going up.

The Turkey Shoot

THE LONGER we stayed around Saipan the more apparent it became that the enemy was getting ready to hit us with everything he had. No large-scale aerial attacks had been launched at us, but snoopers of all kinds were more numerous. On one patrol Jim Stewart shot down a Judy, while my division was chasing a Betty off to the other side of the task force. When we finally spotted the Betty it passed over us on a course opposite to ours with about a two-thousand-foot altitude advantage, so that we were never able to catch it. Obviously the Japs knew exactly where we were and what we were up to.

Once our troops were ashore on Saipan, there could be no backing out, no matter how slow the going and how tough the opposition, which was very, very tough. Evidently the Japs had loaded this island with crack troops, with the idea of throwing our landing forces back into the sea while their fleet steamed up to hit us from behind. Their determined resistance slowed down the progress of our men ashore, while their land-based bombers harassed our support craft and landing

parties with night attacks which began at sunset each
evening. Scheduled air attacks and landings on Tinian
and Guam had to be delayed in order to give our troops
on Saipan more support in their precarious position.

This gave the Japs the opening they had been await-
ing for nearly two years. They now had us committed to
the support of landing operations too important to be
abandoned, more than a thousand miles west of our out-
ermost support base at Eniwetok. They had us out-
flanked from the north with a chain of airfields from
the Empire through the Bonins, and from the south
they were staging in planes to Guam from the Philippines via Palau and Yap. Their big airfield on Guam's
Orote peninsula, still operational in spite of all our ef-
forts, was only one hundred and seventeen miles from
Aslito airfield on Saipan, which they were defending
tooth and nail from our hard-pressed landing forces.
That was the setup when it was reported that the Jap
fleet was on its way east at high speed to hit us.

The resulting tactical situation was handled brilliantly. Instead of letting themselves be drawn out to
meet the impending threat from the west and leaving
our troops ashore unprotected and vulnerable, our high
command outguessed the Jap admirals and kept the task
force close enough to Saipan and Guam for our fighter
patrols to cover the airfields on these islands. Other
fighter patrols were stationed to the westward to meet
any Jap planes as they came in. The Jap strategy, which
our admirals correctly anticipated, was to launch their
planes as soon as their carriers were within airplane

range of our fleet, then to retire at top speed to the west, so that by the time their first wave hit us their carriers would already be beyond range of any pursuing aircraft we might launch. After hitting our fleet, the Jap planes were to fly on and land at Rota and Guam, where they could refuel, rearm, and hit us again and again. Land-based twin-engined torpedo bombers which they staged in from the south were also to hit us at the same time.

If this plan worked out the way the enemy hoped, our aircraft carriers would be sunk or knocked out of commission, leaving our task force without aerial protection. Then the Japanese fleet would steam in for the long awaited surface engagement with its carriers intact, which would give the enemy every advantage in a one-sided battle. If our fleet stayed to fight under such circumstances it would be sunk. Retreat would mean abandoning our forces ashore to certain destruction. No further offensive operations would be possible for us until we could replace our carriers and amphibious vessels, and retrain thousands of assault troops to replace those who would be lost. It would be a disastrous defeat which, if we could recover from it at all, would extend the war by years.

As the Japanese fleet units converged on us from the west one of our submarines torpedoed an enemy aircraft carrier. This gave us some definite indications as to the location of the enemy fleet and the probable date of the attack: June 18. On that date we braced ourselves for the expected attack, but it did not come. That night we steamed far to the westward at high speed and

launched a long-range scouting search several hours before dawn, but still there was no contact with the enemy.

The nineteenth of June brought another of those days
of perfect visibility which occur so frequently around
the Marianas. Again there was a high thin overcast
which formed a white background perfect for spotting
airplanes. This was a day that I had been training for
almost constantly for nearly nine years. This time I selected the combat air patrol which I thought would be
in the air ready and waiting for the Jap aerial assault
when it arrived, for this was one free-for-all that I did
not intend to miss.

My guess was that the first waves of enemy planes
would strike around ten o'clock in the morning. We had
a twelve-plane flight scheduled to take off at eight
o'clock for a three-hour patrol. My division had missed
the daylight fighter sweep and had not made a kill since
Palau, nearly three months before; today I was going to
get it into the air while the shooting was going on.

The dawn patrols encountered no opposition and
everything was still quiet when we were launched at
eight o'clock to relieve them. Our three divisions cruised
around over the task group for over an hour before we
were alerted, when one division was dispatched to
Guam in response to a call for help from another air
patrol over that island. Upon their arrival they found no
friendly planes in sight, but were immediately jumped
by eight or ten Zekes. Our four planes managed to shoot
their way out, knocking off five Zekes in the process,
but two of our planes were pretty badly shot up, so

that they had to be taken aboard immediately upon their return. Jim Bowie was unable to lower his landing flaps, and as a result his plane ended up in the barriers with a bent propeller.

Since this left us with only eight planes in the air, the Air Officer, Al Gurney, decided to relieve our patrol by launching twelve other planes. My heart sank as I heard this news over the radio, for we had been in the air only two hours and still had enough fuel left for a fight. But orders were orders, and down we spiralled toward the landing circle.

Back aboard, I hurried down to the ready room while our planes were being refuelled and respotted for take-off. I barely had time to get out of my flight gear when the general alarm was sounded. Al Masters stuck his head through the door and gave us the news.

"This is *it*, gang! Many large bogies coming in from the west—several hundred planes!"

Cursing the luck which had caught me on deck at such a time, I grabbed my flight gear and put it on as I ran back along the flight deck, dodging the planes which were already taking off. The twelve standby planes were already manned by the pilots scheduled to make the third flight, but behind these there was a thirteenth plane refuelled and ready to go. As I ducked under the wing of one plane the pilot gunned his engine to taxi across into takeoff position. The propeller blast caught me and blew me straight toward the whirling propeller of another plane. I dropped to the deck, but still the blast rolled me toward sure death in the propeller. Just a few feet short of it my hip bounced into an arresting gear cable, which I grabbed and hung onto in a cold sweat until two plane handlers dragged me out from in front of that whirling scimitar.

There was no time to reflect on this close call, for other danger was approaching at high speed overhead. Climbing into the cockpit of the last fighter on deck, I plugged in my radio earphones. The jumbled medley of excited calls told me that the other patrols had already engaged the enemy. Looking back over my shoulder I saw a group of long white streamers trailing across the sky from the west. These were condensation trails from the exhaust gases of enemy planes approaching at high altitude. As I watched these vapor trails I saw others converging on them from a different angle as our fighters came in to intercept them. For a moment there was a confused tangle of white trails, then long black plumes started curling down as the burning airplanes began to fall.

Finally the last plane ahead of me roared up the deck and into the air. Taxiing into the takeoff spot, I waited for Al Gurney to give me the signal to go. Instead he signalled to the plane handlers to put chocks under my plane's wheels, and gave me the sign to cut my switches. I roared a protest which he must have heard even over the noise of the engine, but he shook his head obstinately and repeated the signal to stop the engine.

Almost beside myself with rage and frustration, I cut the engine and trudged back up the deck to the ready room.

"What's the matter with Gurney?" I demanded of Al Masters. "Has he gone crazy?"

"No, he just wants to save that plane until we can bring up the rest of the fighters from the hangar deck," answered Masters. "Don't worry; we'll get you off in a few minutes."

"In a few minutes we'll have Jap dive bombers all over us!" I retorted. "Didn't you see those vapor trails?"

"No! My God, are they that close?"

"Go take a look for yourself. They're not more than twenty miles away!"

Meanwhile the remaining Hellcats were being brought up from the hangar deck as fast as the elevators could be operated. While I was protesting about missing the last flight, Nooy seized the opportunity to climb into the first plane on the catapult. Racing two other ensigns, I beat them to the second plane and taxied up to the catapult behind Nooy. Behind us I heard the destroyer screen opening up with five-inch guns; the enemy was already within shooting distance.

As Nooy was catapulted I watched him make a quick turn to the left at low altitude instead of the standard slow climb to the right. Evidently he had already spotted enemy planes. After what seemed an interminable delay my plane was hooked up to the catapult. At that moment the *Cabot's* stern 40-mm. guns went into action. Without even testing my engine I gave the launching signal, and was immediately snapped off the deck and into the air.

Banking to the left, I headed downwind to get out

of the task group as quickly as possible before our own ships shot me down. The enemy planes, I knew, would be coming in upwind from the west. By heading in the opposite direction from which the attack was coming, I would be less likely to be fired on by mistake. As I passed the stern of the *Cabot* I could see the ship's AA batteries flashing and their big 40-mm. tracer shells streaking past me. Looking up in the direction of the firing I saw two airplanes diving toward the task force. One was already afire and as I watched, it attempted a suicide dive on the *Cabot*, whose anti-aircraft fire soon splashed it. The other plane also was hit during its dive. It burst into flames and came down in a flat spin so close to my plane that I had to change course to avoid it. Why I wasn't shot down at the same time will always be a mystery to me.

Black puffs of smoke from five-inch AA shells filled the area I was flying through. Realizing that I was in a tight spot, I almost bent the throttle in my anxiety to get clear. Off to the south I saw Nooy's plane climbing toward the east. I soon joined him, and together we headed east out of gun range from the task group. One by one the others joined us until we had a formation of eight planes.

Someone spotted another formation approaching the task group: "Tallyho! Large bogey at ten o'clock up!"

In the direction indicated I saw a group of fifteen or twenty airplanes approaching from the east about ten miles away. They were flying a tight formation of stepped-down V's, which indicated that they were multi-place dive bombers or torpedo planes with rear-seat gunners. Starting a fast climb, I led the others into attack position. A few quick glances around showed no fighter escort. This would be easy pickings.

For once I was in the perfect position every fighter pilot dreams about, with plenty of time to get lined up for an overhead or high side run and no fighter opposition to bother us. It was too good to be true, which it wasn't. Even before I could start a run on the formation a half mile below me I could see the white wing insignia against the dark background of the ocean below, which identified them as friendly planes. On closer inspection they proved to be a group of our own SBD's. I learned later that these had been launched from one of the big carriers to get them off of the deck and out of harm's way when the expected attack arrived.

We returned to the vicinity of our task group and chased every airplane we could find for nearly an hour, but not one proved to be Japanese. Evidently our combat air patrols had done their work well, for no other enemy planes got through to the task group that morning. Bitterly disappointed, we were brought back aboard without having fired a gun in the biggest aerial battle of the war.

That battle, which was afterward referred to as the Marianas Turkey Shoot, cost the Japanese three hundred and fifty-three airplanes. Our own forces lost twenty-one planes, from which eight pilots were rescued. Pilots of my squadron shot down twenty-eight enemy planes that day without the loss of a single airplane or pilot. Eight of them had torn into a formation of about fifty Zekes and Judys with such enthusiasm and abandon that one pilot reported counting at least fifteen Jap planes going down in flames at one time, and seven parachutes in the air.

It was a great day for our side. The Jap attack had been smashed, and our invasion forces ashore had been saved. The Japanese had been dealt a blow from which they were never to recover, for the loss of their carrier air groups broke the back of their naval air power, and they were never again able to go on the offensive. Later on we were to realize that this had been one of the decisive battles of the war.

Just to make the day perfect, that evening we received a message from our task group commander:

> CONGRATULATIONS YOU WERE TOPS IN OUR LEAGUE TODAY.

The "Meataxe Squadron" had finally lived up to its name.

The Eastern Philippines

BEFORE WE COULD start out in pursuit of the Japanese carriers from which their ill-fated attack had been launched, our own carriers had to steam upwind to recover their own airplanes. With the easterly trade winds, this gave the enemy a good start for safety.

The Jap carrier force had undoubtedly turned tail, writing off its pilots as expendable, and headed back downwind to the west as fast as it could go. At the time their planes were launched the enemy carriers were at least five hundred miles from Saipan, and by the time we could turn into the wind and recover our flights after the aerial attack the Jap fleet probably had a head start on us of at least four hours, which would put them another hundred miles away to the west of us. With a lead of five or six hundred miles they might get almost to the Philippines before we could catch them. Perhaps that was what they planned—to draw us out within range of their land-based bombers, then to hit us with their remaining aircraft carriers at the same time. Nevertheless our admirals started the pursuit as soon as the last fighter plane was back aboard.

During their retreat the Japs had two distinct advantages. They did not have to slow down to refuel, having topped off before launching. In addition, they did not have to turn back into the wind to launch or recover search aircraft, as we did. They knew where we were, but we could not be sure whether their retiring course would be west to the Philippines, south to Palau, or north to Japan, which meant that every few hours we had to turn back into the easterly wind in order to keep search planes in the air. Our escorting destroyers were also running low on fuel.

In spite of all this, our task groups slowly closed on the fleeing Jap force, and about midafternoon on June 20 our search planes made contact. Their first reports gave the position of the enemy fleet as two hundred and fifty miles west of us, but later calculations indicated that the Jap carriers, which were our primary targets, were considerably farther ahead of their screening destroyers and cruisers. The decision was made to attack immediately, and a large striking group of dive bombers, fighters, and torpedo planes took off from the *Essex*-class carriers and headed west. Shortly afterward a second attack wave was launched, about three hours before sunset. The *Cabot* was called on to supply only four Avengers, our other planes being held for subsequent strikes. Everyone realized that these pilots would probably be unable to deliver their attack and return before sunset, and that any unforeseen delay would mean night landings.

Those who are inclined to criticize our high command

for the decision to attack immediately, instead of continuing the chase all night in order to hit the enemy at dawn the next day, should first consider the factors involved. In the first place, our destroyers were so low on fuel that an overnight chase would have left them helpless to assist in a major surface engagement, and we could not slow down to refuel them. Secondly, in order to maintain contact with the enemy during the night we would have had to launch additional search planes every few hours, further delaying the chase and increasing the enemy's lead, always with the possibility of losing contact in the darkness, which would have meant another search the next morning. Worse yet, we were already within range of land-based bombers from Yap and Palau, and an overnight run would have brought us close enough to the Philippines for the Japs to hit us from several land bases at once. Obviously it was best to hit them while we had the chance.

The four planes from our carrier which went in with the first attack wave each carried four 500-pound bombs. What happened to these pilots and their crews is typical of what many others went through that night.

It was after four o'clock when they took off, and contact with the Japanese rear-guard destroyers was not made until six-thirty that evening. These ships opened fire on our planes as they passed overhead in search of the Jap carriers, which were about twenty miles beyond to the northwest. Dive bombers from another carrier led the attack. Our torpedo planes, led by their twenty-four-year-old squadron commander,

Lt. Wood, started a glide-bombing run from eighty-five hundred feet on a *Shokaku*-class carrier. It had no planes on deck and was as yet unhit. A few Zeros made passes at our pilots during their approach, but were driven off by the rear gunners. Wood's string of four 500-pound bombs straddled the Jap carrier, with two hits on the stern, setting it afire. His wingman, "Beast" Russell, also scored two hits near the stern, causing a secondary explosion.

The other two pilots, seeing this carrier already afire, selected a nearby *Kongo*-class battleship for their target. Lt. (jg) D. W. Smith scored with two of his bombs and Ensign Jimmy Jones, Jr. hit this ship with one bomb. Pilots from other carriers were bombing the rest of the frantically circling Jap warships with equal determination, scoring hits on at least fourteen ships. The attack was completed in about fifteen minutes and our planes were on their way back at about seven o'clock. At this time it was still daylight at the target, but where we were, the sun had already gone down below the horizon. Aboard the *Cabot* and the other carriers which were standing by to recover the returning planes the tension increased as nearly two hours passed with no word from the attack group. The last faint rays of the sun had faded, and there was no moon. Off to the southward a flicker of lightning flashed intermittently.

It was nearly nine o'clock before our radar picked up the returning planes to the westward. At the same time several enemy planes were reported to be in our vicinity only a few miles south, apparently having trailed our planes back from the Jap carriers. Here was the situation which every pilot dreads more than any other: these enemy planes could turn on their lights and mingle undetected with our returning aircraft, shooting our planes down from point-blank range. Furthermore, any ship which showed a light would be a perfect target for a strafing, bombing, or torpedo attack by the intruding Jap planes. Old-timers aboard shook their heads gloomily. It looked as if we were going to have to write off our pilots in order to save our carriers, just as the Japs had done the previous day in a vain attempt to save theirs. All the tired, desperate pilots circling above us were literally between the devil and the deep black sea, for a forced landing even in broad daylight is so dangerous that most pilots prefer to bail out rather than attempt a water landing in darkness on the open ocean. Radio conversations told us that some pilots were hopefully heading for the false beacon of the distant lightning. It was heartbreaking to hear them. We were facing the worst disaster in the history of U.S. Naval Aviation.

Then an amazing, incredible thing happened. Our blacked-out ships began to turn on their lights—red truck lights on the outer screen, bright flashing lights to identify the individual carriers, glow-lights to outline the flight decks, vertical searchlight beams and starshells to mark our position for those still too far out to see us—friend and foe alike. We stood open-mouthed on the deck for a moment at the sheer audacity of asking the Japs to come and get us, then a spontaneous cheer went up. To Hell with the Japs around us! Let them come in if they dared. Japs or no Japs, the Navy was taking care of its own; *our* pilots were not expendable!

The scenes which followed will be vividly remembered by those who saw them for the rest of their lives. All around us airplanes whose fuel tanks had run dry were landing on the black water in the searchlight beams from the destroyers. Many planes got aboard with their last few gallons of gasoline. The first plane to land aboard the *Cabot* was a Hellcat from another ship. Next came a Helldiver which looked so big that his winglights appeared to project beyond the edges of our narrow flight deck. Lt. Wood came back aboard for a perfect landing with only five gallons left in his reserve fuel tank. Another Helldiver came in too fast and crashed into the barrier wires. It was pushed over the side to make room for other planes, while the barriers were replaced in record time by our flight deck repair crew. Deck crashes on other carriers resulted when pilots were unable to take a wave-off as their tanks ran dry in the last few yards of their approach. These accidents, marked by the billowing flames of gasoline fires, temporarily jammed flight decks so that the remaining airborne pilots had to land aboard other carriers. The *Cabot* recovered more planes than she was theoretically supposed to be able to accommodate. Herculean tasks were performed that night which we would have considered impossible a few hours earlier. Bravery and self-sacrifice were commonplace, and many good men died that night trying to help their friends in the air back to a safe landing.

Finally the sands of time ran out, and the last plane aloft had used its few remaining pints of fuel to make a power-stall landing into the sea ahead of a destroyer. All that night the destroyers cruised back and forth picking up survivors. God was with us again, for there was an unusual flat calm which made forced landings easier and facilitated search and rescue operations.

During the night the task force cruised toward the scene of the battle, picking up survivors en route. The next morning searching planes combed the entire area, spotting the yellow pneumatic life-rafts and directing destroyers out to pick up their occupants. All that day we cruised along the route taken by our attacking planes the day before, and still the seas were calm and flat. Pilots were picked up right and left, until our personnel losses were only a small fraction of what we had feared the night before.

Of our own four airplanes on this strike, Wood and Russell landed back aboard and Jones made a crash landing on another carrier. Smith and his crew were picked up by a destroyer two hours after they landed at sea. Other pilots were picked up almost twenty-four hours later. The Navy left nothing undone which could possibly contribute to the rescue of any man.

We learned later that it was Admiral Marc Mitscher himself who ordered the lights turned on that night, even though he was warned that it meant exposing the fleet to probable attack. It was reported that Japanese planes were seen inside the task force, and that one Jap even tried to land aboard one of our carriers, but was waved off. The Japs may have been so flabbergasted by the sudden appearance in a darkened ocean of so many lighted ships that they retired in confusion; in any case no aerial attacks were made on our ships.

Some idea of the confusion which reigned that night may be gathered from the experience of The Beast, who cruised around over the formation, dodging other airplanes, until he found a CVL where the *Cabot* was reported to be.

"It looked so small that I decided not to risk a night landing," he said afterward, "so I stalled around looking for the biggest CV I could find, and landed on it."

As he climbed out of his Avenger, one of the plane handlers greeted him with, "That was a beautiful landing, Mr. Russell—just like daytime!"

"How'd you know my name?" demanded The Beast. "What ship is this?"

"Why the *Cabot*, of course!" was the answer. "What did you think it was?"

"That's all I want to know!" answered The Beast, whereupon he knelt and kissed the deck affectionately.

How did our pilots feel about this last-minute reprieve? Their reactions are a fitting commentary on the *esprit de corps* of Naval Aviation.

Had they thought that they would be left to shift for themselves when they came back in the dark with enemy planes around? They laughed at the idea.

"We knew you'd pick us up," they said. "*Japanese* pilots may be expendable, but *we* don't do things that way!"

End of a Battle

ON THE MORNING after the night action we were still cruising at high speed in pursuit of the retreating enemy fleet. Our search planes finally located what was left of the Japanese force, limping toward Luzon with several ships trailing oil, about three hundred and fifty miles northwest of us. A strike was ordered. This time CVL's were to be in on it, because of the heavy plane losses suffered by the bigger carriers whose air groups had made the water landings the night before. The *Cabot's* air group was to lead the attack, and I was designated as the strike leader.

We had twelve Hellcats loaded with 500-pound armor-piercing bombs, and our fighters were to accompany sixteen Helldivers carrying 1000-pound bombs and twelve Avengers loaded with torpedoes.

After we manned our planes we sat waiting for the task group to reverse course and head into the wind for launching, but nearly half an hour passed with no change in our steady course to the northwest. Going downwind there was very little breeze over the deck and before long we were sweating under the morning sun. I was excited over the prospect of finally getting a crack at a Jap carrier with a bomb, and also looking forward to a chance to test my theory that an aircraft carrier could be set afire by fighters with a well-coordinated strafing attack.

While I was sitting in the cockpit re-checking my navigation Steve Kona climbed up on my wing and looked over my shoulder with a quizzical grin. Even before he spoke I knew what he was going to say.

"Captain," he said, "we can't make it that far with these bombs and get back."

"I know it, Steve," I answered, and indicated a point on my plotting board several dozen miles short of our return destination. "I figure we can get back about to here."

"Then what do we do?"

"We'll all land and tie our rubber boats in a circle and wait for them to pick us up. There's not much wind and the sea is smooth. We shouldn't have any trouble."

"We're getting awfully close to the Philippines," he reminded me. "Suppose they don't come and pick us up?"

"Don't worry—they always pick us up."

"Well—I hope you're right!"

Just then a yeoman walked up with a message chalked on a wooden blackboard. He held it up while I copied down the information: *add fifty to seventy-five miles distance to Jap carriers.* This meant a flight of over four hundred miles—well beyond our radius of action with such a heavy load. There was no longer even a faint hope of our being able to make it to the target and back. Kona grinned at me silently.

"Don't tell the others," I told him.

"I won't have to," he answered. "They can add."

I patted him on the shoulder, and he stuck his hand into the cockpit.

"Good luck!" he said, as we shook hands.

"Same to you, and don't worry!"

He grinned again and was gone. I sat alone in the shimmering heat, wondering if this time they could afford to come and pick us up. Snoopers had been around us all day, even a big four-engined Emily which one patrol had shot down. It looked like a real trap was being set, with the enemy task force as the bait to lure us on. Our high command could do exactly as the Japs had done the day before—weigh the risk, figure the cost, launch the planes to do as much damage as they could, and write them off as an expendable battle cost. The longer I studied my chart board the more I expected just that—and I knew that no one could justly condemn our admirals for launching a strike under such circumstances.

Not long afterward the ship began to heel over as the task group started a simultaneous turn back into the easterly breeze. I began to prime my engine for a quick start. Suddenly a group of ordnancemen appeared and started unshackling the bombs under our wings. The squadron duty officer came running up and gave me the reason: "The strike has been called off. The Admiral has ordered all planes to search for survivors instead!"

I breathed a fervent sigh of relief. A short time later we were in the air—not on a one-way trip as we had expected, but over our retiring task force on a homeward course.

We had been airborne only a few minutes before the *Cabot's* radar picked up a bogey to the south. My division was vectored out to make the interception, which was a classic of fighter direction. The fighter director was Lt. "Wary" Werrenrath, who had taken over the job after Pat Rooney had been detached to form his own fighter squadron. Werrenrath had a sixth sense for bogies; he could spot an enemy plane farther than any fighter director I ever knew. This time he sent us toward the Philippines.

"Hello, Topaz One-One, this is Topaz Base: vector one-nine-five, liner!"

"Topaz One-One, on vector," I acknowledged. "What size bogey?"

"Single plane, distance ninety, angels fifteen. Go to angels eighteen."

This meant that the bogey was ninety miles away at an altitude of about fifteen thousand feet, and that we were to climb to eighteen thousand feet so that we would have an altitude advantage of three thousand feet—ideal for an overhead or high side attack. We climbed accordingly, still on the same course.

I kept waiting for a change in vector, but Wary kept us on the same heading. I knew that he would try to put us in position to have the morning sun behind us to blind the enemy rear gunners, which would mean that we would find the bogey to our right. This would give Wilson, who was leading the right-hand section, first crack at the Jap and a chance to raise his number of four aerial victories to a total of five, which would qualify him for the much-coveted designation of "ace."

Whoever started this ace business during the First World War certainly laid up a lot of trouble for the squadron commanders in my day. Our pilots would run any risk to make their first kill, I knew, and I had soon found that they were even more hell-bent on scoring their fifth. Once they had five planes to their credit they usually settled down and stopped behaving like the Mohawk Indian warriors whose war-dance was painted in gaudy colors on the *Cabot's* open bridge.

With this in mind, I gradually eased my section away from Wilson's so that he would not have to hurry his attack in order to get in ahead of my wingman Nooy, who was his room-mate and who was also eager to run up his score.

"Bogey ahead about ten miles," said Wary. "Should be about one o'clock down."

Almost immediately Wilson spotted the bogey and called, "Tallyho! One Betty at two o'clock down!"

"Go get him!" I cried, and Wilson started a high side approach.

Wilson was in perfect position and made a beautiful run, diving at an angle of about sixty degrees out of the sun onto the unsuspecting Jap. The Betty was about three miles to my right and below us when Wilson opened fire. I saw no flames, but the big Jap plane suddenly went into a steep diving turn to the right. Obviously it was hard hit.

On seeing this, Nooy cut under me to intercept it. I knew that if he set it afire after Wilson had hit it first there would inevitably be an argument over who made the kill. The only way to prevent this was to beat Nooy to the punch, and with this in mind I poured on the coal and cut inside of his turn, opening fire at extreme range. The Betty's wing tanks burst into flames and it continued in its steep diving turn. As I pulled up over it Nooy opened fire and knocked off its right wing. Hancock followed with a run from astern which brought more flames from the stricken giant.

It was like shooting down an airliner. I watched its death dive, unable to take my eyes away, until it struck the smooth water in a sickening crash that scattered fragments of the plane for hundreds of yards ahead of the point of impact.

"Splashed one Betty!" said Nooy over the radio.

"Any survivors?" asked the *Cabot's* radio.

"No survivors," I answered, still watching the flaming oil slick three miles below us.

"Reverse vector," directed Wary.

That was the only order he gave us for the course back. With a downhill run we cruised at high speed and after about twenty minutes sighted the task force dead ahead. Werrenrath had given us only two vectors, one for the interception and one for the return.

The rest of the day was spent searching for survivors along the course taken by the strikes launched the day before. Many pilots were picked up who would have been lost otherwise, including several group and squadron commanders with invaluable experience.

The following day Wilson, flying as a substitute for another pilot who was unable to fly with his own division, shot down another Betty which, by approaching in a fast climb, had managed to evade the outer patrols and get in over the task force. Wilson finally caught up with this snooper at an altitude of over twenty thousand feet—so high that when he first hit it the big plane flamed only momentarily before the fires were blown out. Wilson made repeated runs on this plane, but could not set it afire until he had battered it down to about fifteen thousand feet, where it finally fell apart and crashed.

It was not until late the next afternoon that we sighted the big fleet oilers sent out to refuel our ships. They were a welcome sight, for we now felt that we were safe from the danger of being forced into a surface engagement with insufficient fuel for a running battle.

The next day we were back on the job of giving aerial support to the invasion troops ashore on Saipan. Harassing attacks on our own landing craft by scattered groups of enemy planes continued. These attacks were usually launched from Rota or Guam by planes staged in at night from Yap or Iwo Jima. The enemy even managed to keep a sizable number of fighters in operation on Guam.

One morning we received an urgent call to send all available fighters to cover the rescue submarine operating off Guam. At that time we had all but two of our fighters tied up either on support strikes or being refuelled and rearmed. With Wilson in the other plane, the two of us made an unopposed flight to Guam. We spotted the rescue submarine on the surface when we were nearly twenty miles away from it. The sub was cruising along about a dozen miles west of Guam's Orote peninsula, where the Japs had their main airfield on Guam. There was no doubt that it could be easily spotted even by observers on the shore, for the sea was calm and smooth.

"Fighter cover approaching," I notified the sub commander by radio.

"We see only two planes," was the answer. "When will the others arrive?"

"Only two planes available," I replied.

"What is this, a suicide mission? Don't you know that there are enemy planes around?"

"Yes, we know it," I answered. "Please warn us if you see any approaching."

"Wilco. We have four dunked aviators aboard. When are you going to send us some more business?"

"Any time now. We'll probably be your next guests, if those Zekes spot us."

"We're not worried about airplanes, but keep a sharp lookout for periscopes. While we're surfaced we'd be an easy shot for an enemy sub."

For over four hours we cruised around over the submarine in plain view of the shore. I could even see enemy shipping in Apra Harbor. Why the Japs did not come out and nail us I will never be able to understand, but the most logical explanation is that they thought that our two planes were merely decoys sent to lure them into a trap. In any event we were not attacked, and after being relieved on station by two divisions of Hellcats from another carrier we returned to the *Cabot* without further incident.

This was the last of our action off Saipan, for our task group was relieved by another so that we could retire to rearm and replenish our supplies. This time we did not have to go all the way back to Majuro, but headed for the big lagoon of Eniwetok, where a new naval base had been established after the conquest of the atoll.

En route to Eniwetok the following message was received from our Fleet Commander, Admiral Spruance:

THE ACTION OF PAST FEW DAYS HAS AGAIN DEMONSTRATED THAT THE JAPANESE FLEET IS NOT YET READY TO ACCEPT ACTION WITH OUR FLEET X ENEMY AIR ATTACKS ON TF. 58 ON 19TH WERE OVERCOME WITH TRIFLING DAMAGE TO OUR SHIPS AND WITH MAXIMUM LOSSES OF ENEMY AIRCRAFT X THESE RESULTS WERE ACCOMPLISHED BY SPLENDID WORK BY OUR FIGHTER PILOTS, EXCELLENT AA GUNNERY BY SHIPS AND SKILLFUL MANEUVERING BY UNITS UNDER ATTACK X LATE AFTERNOON AIR ATTACKS ON 20TH ON THE RETREATING ENEMY FLEET WERE EXECUTED BY OUR AIR GROUPS AT MORE THAN EXTREME RANGE WITH GREAT

SKILL AND BRAVERY X OUR LOSSES IN AIRCRAFT WERE REGRETTABLY LARGE BECAUSE OF THE LONG FLIGHTS AND NIGHT LANDINGS INVOLVED BUT HEAVY DAMAGE WAS INFLICTED ON THE ENEMY FLEET BY OUR ATTACKS X WE HAVE PREVENTED INTERFERENCE WITH OUR AMPHIBIOUS FORCES IN THE MARIANAS BY THE ENEMY FLEET, HAVE WRECKED HIS CARRIER AIR GROUPS, HAVE DAMAGED OR SUNK SOME OF HIS SHIPS AND HAVE FORCED HIS FLEET TO RETREAT PRECIPITATELY WITH CONSEQUENT LOWERING OF HIS MORALE X OUR BATTLESHIPS, CRUISERS AND DESTROYERS ARE GRIEVOUSLY DISAPPOINTED AT NOT BEING ABLE TO ENGAGE BUT THE DISTANCE AT WHICH THE ENEMY WAS PICKED UP, HIS URGENT DESIRE TO GET _AWAY_ AND THE UNFAVORABLE DIRECTION OF THE WIND PREVENTED US FROM CLOSING X BETTER LUCK NEXT TIME X OUR COUNTRY OWES ANOTHER DEBT OF GRATITUDE TO OUR CARRIER AIR GROUPS WHO BORE THE BRUNT OF THE FIGHTING WITH THE EVASIVE ENEMY FLEET AFTER 8 PREVIOUS DAYS OF INTENSIVE AIR OPERATIONS IN THE MARIANAS X WELL DONE TO ALL HANDS.

Sixty-Four to Nothing

EN ROUTE TO ENIWETOK our task group paused long enough to dump its remaining bombs on the Japanese airfield and ground installations on Pagan Island, one of the enemy's staging points between Iwo Jima and Saipan. No airborne opposition was encountered and our air groups suffered no damage. Pagan's defenses were thoroughly wrecked.

From Pagan to Eniwetok the cruise was uneventful, and within a few days we rode at anchor in the big lagoon of our newest island base. While we were here the ship's communications officer again brought up the subject of my orders for detachment, and asked who would relieve me as air group commander. I recommended Lt. Al Mencin, my executive officer and the senior pilot in the air group, but to my disappointment the ship's Air Officer insisted on bringing in a lieutenant commander from another ship as my relief. This officer, although senior to Mencin, was much younger and had far less experience in combat. Upon his arrival I was detached with orders to take the first available air transportation back to Washington.

The small boat which took me from the *Cabot* to the beach was over an hour on the way. As I waved goodbye to the group at the gangway I was filled with mixed feelings of relief and regret, for with this departure I realized that my days as a squadron commander and as a fighter pilot were past. I was going home—and all in one piece. This meant goodbye to general alarms and wave-offs with a near-empty fuel tank, but it also meant farewell to a great group of boys who were already tops in their class.

Although I was still bitter about the way I had been kept on deck during the greatest air battle of the war, I had to admit that I had been lucky in all other respects. My squadron had already set an enviable record without losing a single pilot either operationally or in combat in a half-year of war in the Pacific. Our score of sure kills was sixty-four to nothing, with eight more probables and eight enemy planes destroyed on the ground. We were credited with a total of one hundred and thirteen enemy planes destroyed or damaged, two ships sunk, and seventeen ships damaged. We had lost four planes in water landings due to battle damage, but of the thirty-two pilots who had started out with the squadron when we embarked for the Pacific eight months before, every last man was alive and whole. In operating from half a dozen different carriers my own most serious mishap had been one blown-out tire. Not many pilots had been as consistently lucky.

Ashore at Eniwetok I boarded a NATS transport which took me to Kwajalein, where I could hardly believe my eyes at the amount of construction accomplished in the few months since we had captured the atoll. A few hours later we paused on tiny Johnston Island to refuel, and the next morning the big four-engined Douglas transport eased down at Pearl Harbor.

At Ford Island I stayed overnight at the quarters of Lt. Comdr. Jim Taylor, another ex-cadet who was on the engineering staff of ComAirPac. Jim took me for a swim in the pool at the Tennis Club, put me up overnight, and sent me on my way refreshed. The next day, on the Fourth of July, I arrived by Navy seaplane at the NATS Oakland Terminal and telephoned my wife to tell her that I was back. She greeted me with the words, "Hello, Commander!" and when I begged for an explanation she informed me that through the mysterious grapevine telegraph system known only to navy wives she had learned that my name was on the promotion list of a new ALNAV announcement.

Since the airliner in which I was scheduled to fly to Washington would not leave until late that night I checked into a San Francisco hotel to rest up. After a hot bath I pulled down the shades and was soon fast asleep. Suddenly I was awakened by the persistent clanging of a loud bell. Springing out of bed I fumbled around for several seconds trying to remember where I was and why the general alarm was being sounded. Finally I was sufficiently awake to raise a window shade and locate the source of the "general alarm"—one of San Francisco's famous cable cars was bumping along up the street below me, with the motorman clanging the bell in the traditional manner of his quaint profession. I gave up all thought of sleep in that hotel, and checked in at the airport several hours before my plane was ready to leave.

The next day I was back home with my family after only forty-eight hours of flying from the war which now seemed so distant and unreal that it might well be on another planet.

Upon checking in at the Navy Department I learned that my new assignment was in the Aviation Training Division. Instead of taking the customary period of leave which was given to aviators returning from combat I reported for duty at once, and was soon up to my ears in paper work.

From time to time during the next three months I heard news of my boys' latest exploits—July 4 over Iwo Jima, later in the month over Ulithi and Yap. On the fourth of August they hit Haha Jima, Palau on the seventh, and Mindanao in the first Philippine strikes on the tenth. On the thirteenth of August over Mindanao they shot down twenty-nine planes. On the twenty-first, over Clark Field at Manila, they beat their "Turkey Shoot" record by shooting down twenty-nine enemy planes in one day.

It was on this flight over Clark Field that Nooy, my former wingman, shot down five enemy fighters on one flight while carrying a 500-pound bomb. He got rid of the fifth Jap, after all his ammunition was expended, by flying just over the enemy plane and gradually easing down until he literally flew the Jap into the ground.

Nooy then went on to drop his bomb on an enemy hangar at Clark Field, leaving it afire.

The squadron's last action was on September 24, a long-range strike against enemy shipping in Coron Bay, Visayans. By the first of October the *Cabot* was at anchor in the lagoon of the fleet's new base at Ulithi atoll. A few days later the ship rode out a typhoon, and after this last experience * the squadron disembarked for home with a combat record which still stands.

* *Editor's Note:* However, the replacement group for Fighting Squadron Thirty-One (which contained a nucleus of its original pilots) was engaged in the last aerial fight of the war, as the following press release shows.

U.S. PACIFIC FLEET ADVANCE HEADQUARTERS, GUAM (14 Sept. 1945). The morning of 15 August (East Longitude Date), the day that President Truman announced peace with Japan, found four pilots of Fighting Squadron Forty-Nine from the aircraft carrier U.S.S. *San Jacinto* on the way to their target, airfields in the interior of Japan. Flying with them were four pilots from Fighting Squadron Thirty-One. Halfway to the objective, they encountered the rare sight of fifteen Jap planes in the air. Not only were these Japs in the air but they were attacking four British planes.

Fighting Squadron Forty-Nine jumped to the attack while Thirty-One climbed upstairs to provide cover. Four Japs went down in flames or crashed into the water as a result of the initial attack. But other Japs were now on the tails of Squadron Forty-Nine. So down dove the four fliers from Squadron Thirty-One to take over the fighting and up climbed the men from Forty-Nine to provide top cover.

The fight went on in this manner until twelve of the Japs had been shot down and the others had fled. The action resembled a vertical buzz saw, with our planes rotating from high to low and the Japs feeding in from the side and falling out at the bottom in flames. Not a British or American plane was missing.

To give the fight a storybook finish, as the American planes formed up again, word came over the air that Japan had surrendered.

There were eight *Independence*-class carriers in action during the same period. The records of their original fighting squadrons are as follows:

AIRCRAFT CARRIER	SQUADRON	ENEMY AIRCRAFT SHOT DOWN
CABOT	VF31	147
PRINCETON	VF23 and VF27	95
MONTEREY	VF30 and VF28	68
BATAAN	VF50	60
COWPENS	VF25	48
LANGLEY	VF32	44
BELLEAU WOOD	VF24	30
SAN JACINTO	VF51	9

A total of eighty-one decorations, ranging all the way from the Navy Cross to the Air Medal, were awarded to pilots of the Meataxe Squadron, including eighteen Distinguished Flying Crosses. There were fourteen "Aces" in the squadron who had shot down at least five enemy planes. Nooy was top scorer with fifteen planes shot down, and close behind him were Hawkins and Wirth, each with a total of fourteen aerial victories. For a mustang squadron, my boys had certainly proved that the aviation cadet program had more than paid its freight, and that reserve officers made good fighting men. It was too bad that none of them planned to transfer to the regular Navy after the war, although I had previously recommended most of them for permanent commissions.

These men were typical of the naval aviators who had staved off the Japanese advance in the earlier last-ditch carrier operations and who had sparked our carrier offensive from the Gilberts to Tokyo itself. The importance of their contribution to the ultimate victory cannot be overstressed. Without our aircraft carriers and their carrier air groups there would have been no offensive, no B-29 bases, perhaps even no victory.

LATER ON I was to have the privilege of serving at the advanced headquarters of Fleet Admiral Chester W. Nimitz during the final phases of our carrier attacks on the Japanese home islands in 1945. By the end of July it was obvious that the Japs were on their last legs, for our task force was cruising up and down the Japanese coastline while its battleships shelled cities from close range, and our carrier air groups roamed across the sacred home islands without aerial opposition. Only a few months earlier, similar conditions had presaged the beginning of the end for Germany.

Then on the sixth of August the world was electrified with the announcement that Hiroshima, a Japanese city of 350,000 persons, had been virtually levelled by *one bomb*. When the reports of the first atomic bombing came through on the teletype machines at CINCPAC headquarters the general reaction was one of sheer disbelief. The details were so fantastic that the whole affair sounded like a scientific hoax. Officers who relayed the story to their friends during lunch were laughed at and told that they had been reading too much from the novels of H. G. Wells, who had described atomic bombs in similar terms in his book *The War of the Worlds*.

Gradually it became apparent to even the most skeptical that a new era in warfare had been ushered in with the first use of atomic energy as a weapon. War correspondents clamored for further details, inquiring if this did not mean the end of the naval warfare as well as infantry battles. Subsequent events soon emphasized the significance of the new weapon. Three days later a second atomic bomb was dropped on Nagasaki, destroying one-third of the city. If there was any doubt left in anyone's mind as to the importance of this event, it was quickly dispelled by what followed, for on the same day Russia declared war on Japan and launched attacks into Manchuria and Korea a few minutes later. Russia then revealed that Japan had sought peace through Moscow in mid-June.

With the impact of these triple events the Japanese now had ample face-saving reasons for quitting a lost war, and it did not take them long to make up their minds. Less than forty-eight hours after Russia declared war the beaten Japs broadcast an unofficial acceptance of the Potsdam surrender terms. This was followed by an official peace offer through neutral diplomatic channels the next day. A wild wave of celebrations swept the fleet as hostilities were terminated and victory was assured.

WITH THE INTRODUCTION of atomic warfare, various commentators predicted that aircraft carriers and battleships would soon be as obsolete as the stage-coach. What they overlooked is that the secret of atomic energy is possessed by only two countries, Great Britain and the U.S.A., who happen to possess the only navies of any consequence left on this planet. With Japan's surrender, there is no longer any need to drop atomic bombs. The mere existence of such a weapon should be a sufficient deterrent to the military ambitions of any nation not in on the secret.

It was no doubt necessary to drop at least two atomic bombs in order to demonstrate that the miracle could be duplicated as necessary; but it is conceivable, as General Spaatz hopefully pointed out, that the last atomic bomb has been dropped. In this case, the nature and responsibility of carrier aviation should change very little in the immediate future, for its mobility is a form of insurance against the demonstrated vulnerability of the fixed land base. The immobility of island bases, the "unsinkable aircraft carriers" whose neutralization cost the Japanese their empire, will be an even greater liability in a push-button war. Atomic bombs can be carried easily by the smallest carrier-based planes, giving world-wide flexibility to our nation's defenses. The daring and imagination with which our carrier experts revolutionized naval warfare will find ready application to the new strategy of atomic warfare.

Those who fear the misuse of atomic power forget its potentialities for keeping the peace. If employed intelligently, the new discovery will mean the end of all warfare and an era of world-wide cooperation among a true family of nations. The Navy's greatest chance to serve the nation can be in the role of good-will ambassador to the rest of the world.

The Golden Age of Man may be just around the corner.

About the Author

Robert A. Winston was born in Washington, Indiana, in 1907 and graduated from Indiana University. He worked for *The New York Times* and *The New York News* for five years before starting flight training with the navy in 1935. He flew in fighting squadrons on both coasts and as an instructor at Pensacola, and he wrote about his initial aviation training in *Dive Bomber,* published in 1939 when Winston held the rank of lieutenant. In his second book, *Aces Wild,* he chronicled his experiences in Europe during 1939–40 as a test pilot accompanying a consignment of fighters destined for Finland. Back on active duty in the United States, he served as a flight instructor, then in the public relations office in Washington, D.C. After the attack on Pearl Harbor he was assigned to combat duty in the Pacific, which he recounts in *Fighting Squadron,* published in 1946 when Winston was a commander. At the end of the war he was serving on Admiral Nimitz's staff on Guam. From there he moved to Stockholm, where he served as the naval air attaché.